SpringerBriefs in Computer Science

Series Editors

Stan Zdonik
Peng Ning
Shashi Shekhar
Jonathan Katz
Xindong Wu
Lakhmi C Jain
David Padua
Xuemin (Sherman) Shen
Borko Furht
V.S. Subrahmanian
Martial Hebert
Katsushi Ikeuchi
Bruno Siciliano

For further volumes:
http://www.springer.com/series/10028

Deepak Vohra

JRuby Rails Web
Application Development

 Springer

Deepak Vohra
dvohra09@yahoo.com

ISSN 2191-5768   ISSN 2191-5776 (electronic)
ISBN 978-3-319-03933-6   ISBN 978-3-319-03934-3 (eBook)
DOI 10.1007/978-3-319-03934-3
Springer Cham Heidelberg New York Dordrecht London

Library of Congress Control Number: 2013956201

© The Author(s) 2014
This work is subject to copyright. All rights are reserved by the Publisher, whether the whole or part of the material is concerned, specifically the rights of translation, reprinting, reuse of illustrations, recitation, broadcasting, reproduction on microfilms or in any other physical way, and transmission or information storage and retrieval, electronic adaptation, computer software, or by similar or dissimilar methodology now known or hereafter developed. Exempted from this legal reservation are brief excerpts in connection with reviews or scholarly analysis or material supplied specifically for the purpose of being entered and executed on a computer system, for exclusive use by the purchaser of the work. Duplication of this publication or parts thereof is permitted only under the provisions of the Copyright Law of the Publisher's location, in its current version, and permission for use must always be obtained from Springer. Permissions for use may be obtained through RightsLink at the Copyright Clearance Center. Violations are liable to prosecution under the respective Copyright Law.
The use of general descriptive names, registered names, trademarks, service marks, etc. in this publication does not imply, even in the absence of a specific statement, that such names are exempt from the relevant protective laws and regulations and therefore free for general use.
While the advice and information in this book are believed to be true and accurate at the date of publication, neither the authors nor the editors nor the publisher can accept any legal responsibility for any errors or omissions that may be made. The publisher makes no warranty, express or implied, with respect to the material contained herein.
References to various copyrighted trademarks, servicemarks, marks and registered marks owned by the respective corporations and/or connected subsidiaries may appear in this book. We use the names, logos, and images only in an editorial fashion with no intention of infringement of the trademark.

Printed on acid-free paper

Springer is part of Springer Science+Business Media (www.springer.com)

Abstract

Ruby is one of the top 10 programming languages according to TIOBE index. JRuby is Ruby for the JVM (Java Virtual Machine), a 100 % Java™ implementation of Ruby. The essential difference between Ruby and JRuby is that Ruby runs on the Ruby interpreter and JRuby runs on the JVM. JRuby lets you develop as Ruby and run as Java. JRuby 1.7 supports Ruby 1.9 syntax (except some features) with compatibility level targeting Ruby 1.9.3. Java knowledge is not a pre-requisite to using JRuby.

Several commonly used websites such as LinkedIn™ make use of JRuby. The objective of the brief is to discuss how to develop a Rails web application with JRuby.

What This Brief Covers?

We introduce JRuby. We install JRuby and run a simple script on the JVM. We also invoke Java in a JRuby script. We create a Rails application with JRuby. We create scaffolding for a CRUD application. We package the Rails application with warbler to a WAR file. We deploy the application to JBoss™ application server 7 and to Oracle™ WebLogic Server. We run the JRuby application on WebLogic Server with Oracle™ Database 11g XE as the database. We also run the JRuby application on JBoss application server 7 with MySQL™ database as the database.

What You Need for This Brief?

The brief requires JRuby, version 1.7 is used in the brief. Java 1.7 is also required. For running the Rails application JBoss AS 7 server and Oracle WebLogic Server 12c are used. For database, Oracle Database 11g XE and MySQL databases are used.

Who Is This Brief For?

The target audience of the brief is JRuby developers. The brief is also for Java EE application developers who want to learn about how to package and deploy a JRuby application as a WAR file on a web server. This brief is suitable for professional JRuby developers and also for an intermediate/advanced level course on JRuby.

Deepak Vohra

Contents

Chapter 1
Installing JRuby

In this chapter, we will cover the following topics:

- When to use JRuby
- Installing JRuby

First, we discuss when to use JRuby.

1.1 When to Use JRuby

"JRuby combines the convenience of scripting with the power of the Java platform." (http://www.oracle.com/technetwork/articles/dsl/jruby-141877. html). As a Ruby developer if you want to take advantage of the benefits provided by the Java™ Virtual Machine such as high performance (runtime optimization of byte-code), real multithreading at the OS level with support for multi-core processors (in contrast to the green threads of Ruby, which run at the application level), and integration with the vast archive of Java libraries, JRuby is a suitable candidate. A developer does not have to know any Java to develop a JRuby application. A Rails application may be deployed to any of the application servers as a WAR file just as a Java EE application. JRuby is platform independent which makes it easy to install and migrate.

JRuby is not suitable if using a lot of Ruby gems that require a native C extension, or if requiring some of the un-supported Ruby syntax.

1.2 Installing JRuby

In this section we install JRuby. JRuby is available as an .exe file that runs and starts an install wizard. To run JRuby first we need to install JDK™. JRuby 1.7.0 requires JDK 6 or later. Download and install JDK 7 from http://www.oracle.com/ technetwork/java/javase/downloads/index.html. Set JAVA_HOME

D. Vohra, *JRuby Rails Web Application Development*, SpringerBriefs in Computer Science, DOI 10.1007/978-3-319-03934-3_1, © The Author(s) 2014

environment variable. Add `JAVA_HOME/bin` to `PATH` environment variable. Download the JRuby application for Windows™, `jruby_windows_1_7_0_RC2.exe` or a later version application from `http://jruby.org/`. Double click on the application. The install4j Wizard gets started as shown in Fig. 1.1.

In the **Setup** click on **Next** in the Welcome message dialog as shown in Fig. 1.2.

In **Select Destination Directory** select a **Destination directory** and click on **Next** as shown in Fig. 1.3.

As indicated in Fig. 1.4 the installer will by default setup the `PATH` for JRuby. Click on **Next**.

The JRuby installation gets started as shown in Fig. 1.5.

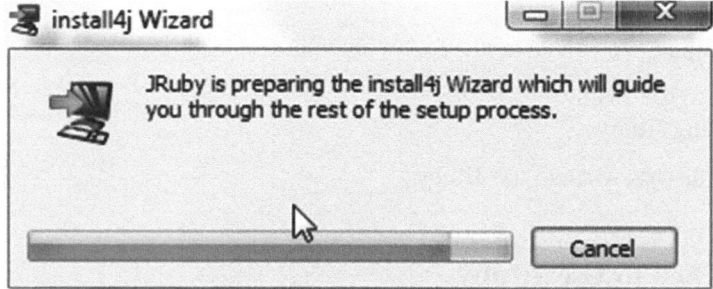

Fig. 1.1 Starting the install4j Wizard

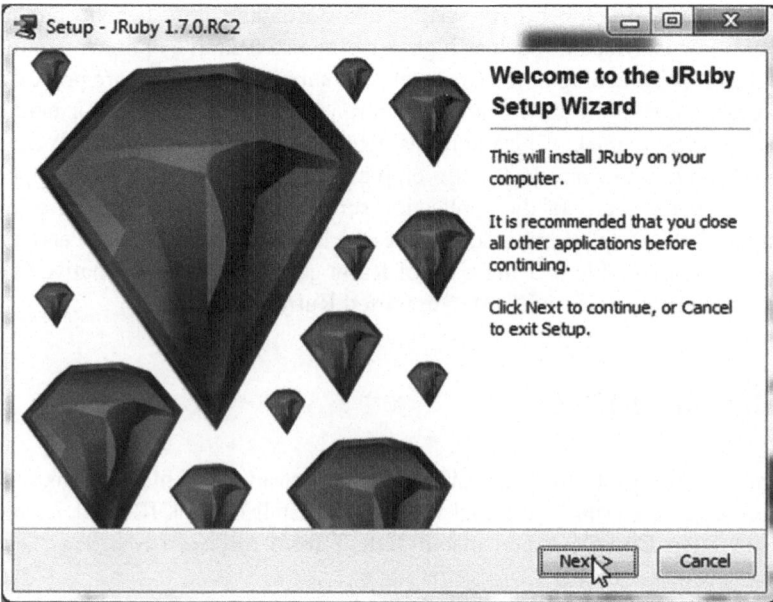

Fig. 1.2 The JRuby Setup Wizard

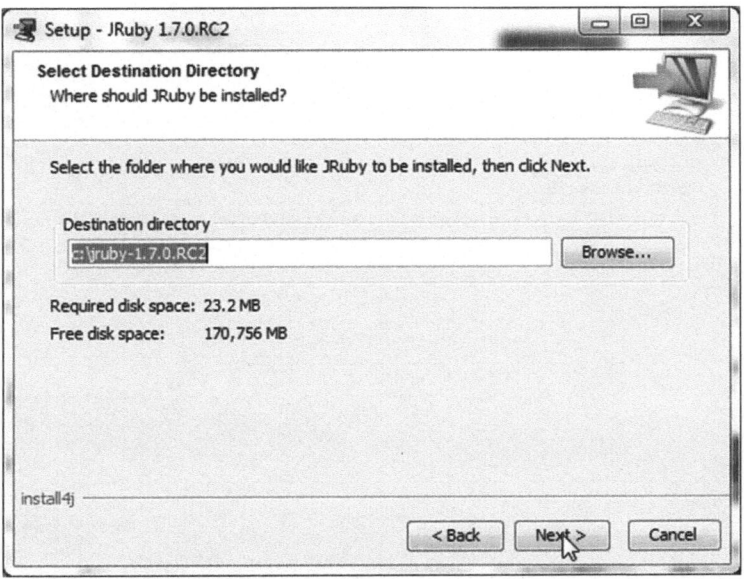

Fig. 1.3 Selecting an installation directory for JRuby

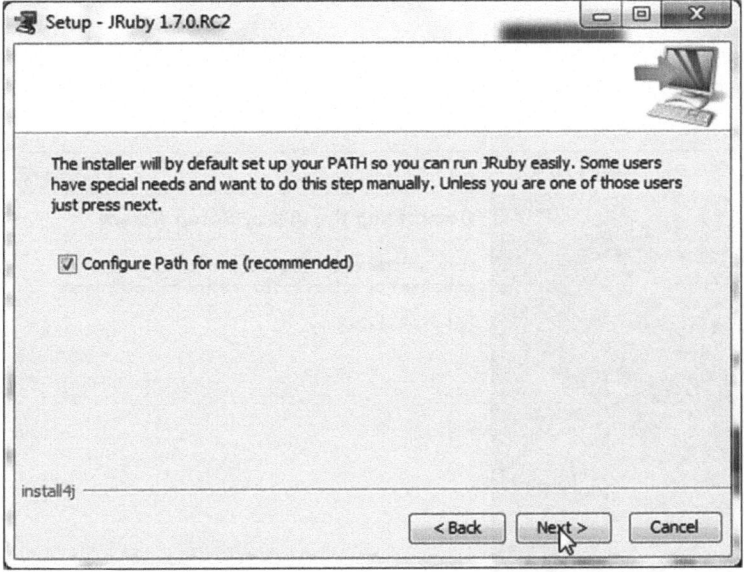

Fig. 1.4 Including JRuby in the PATH environment variable by default

In Completing the JRuby Setup Wizard click on Finish as shown in Fig. 1.6.

JRuby gets installed. If the option to configure PATH was not selected during installation, which automatically does get selected by default, add C:\jruby-1.7.0.RC2\bin to the PATH Environment variable.

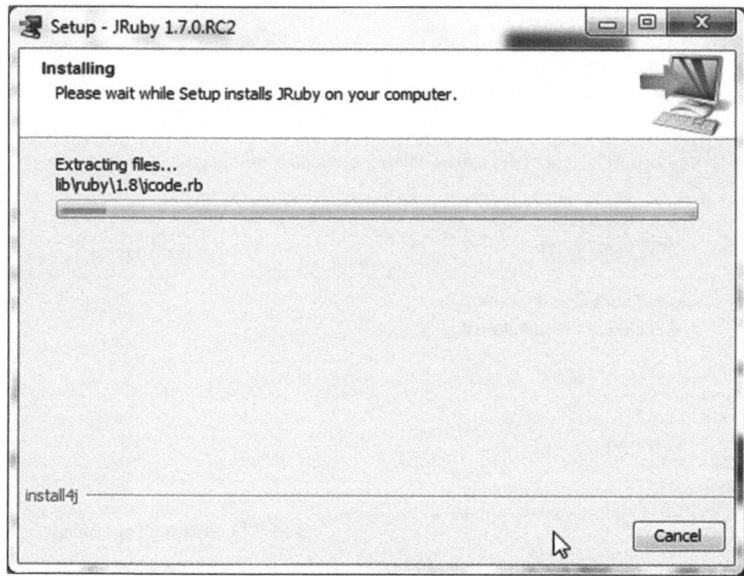

Fig. 1.5 Installing JRuby

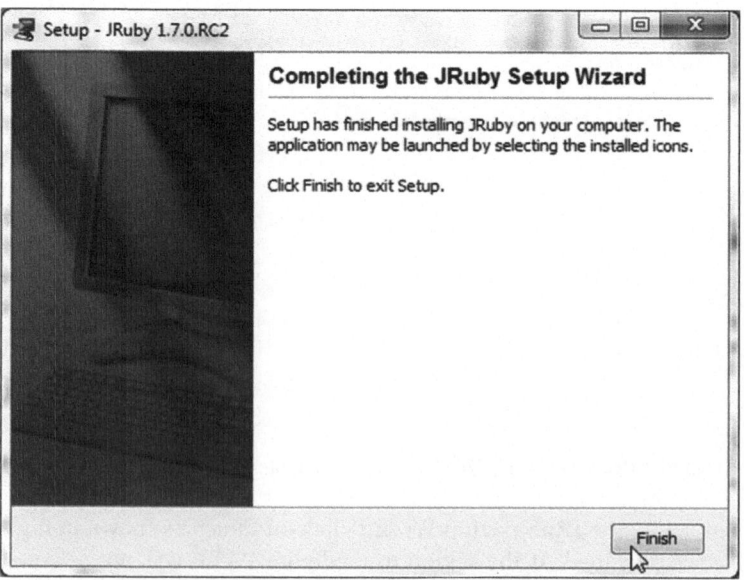

Fig. 1.6 Completing JRuby installation

Administrator: Command Prompt - irb
C:\jruby>jruby -v
jruby 1.7.0.RC2 (1.9.3p203) 2012-10-09 142cc7b on Java HotSpot(TM) Client VM 1.7
.0_05-b05 [Windows 7-x86]
C:\jruby>irb
irb(main):001:0> $a="Hello JRuby"
=> "Hello JRuby"
irb(main):002:0> _

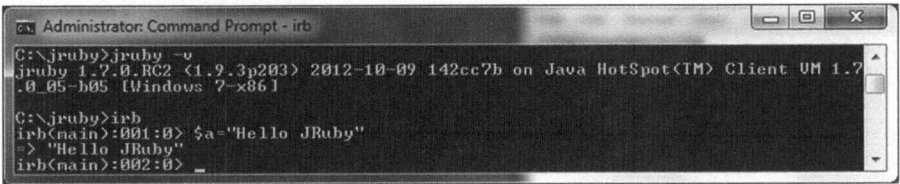

Fig. 1.7 Outputting JRuby version, and running a Ruby statement in the IRB

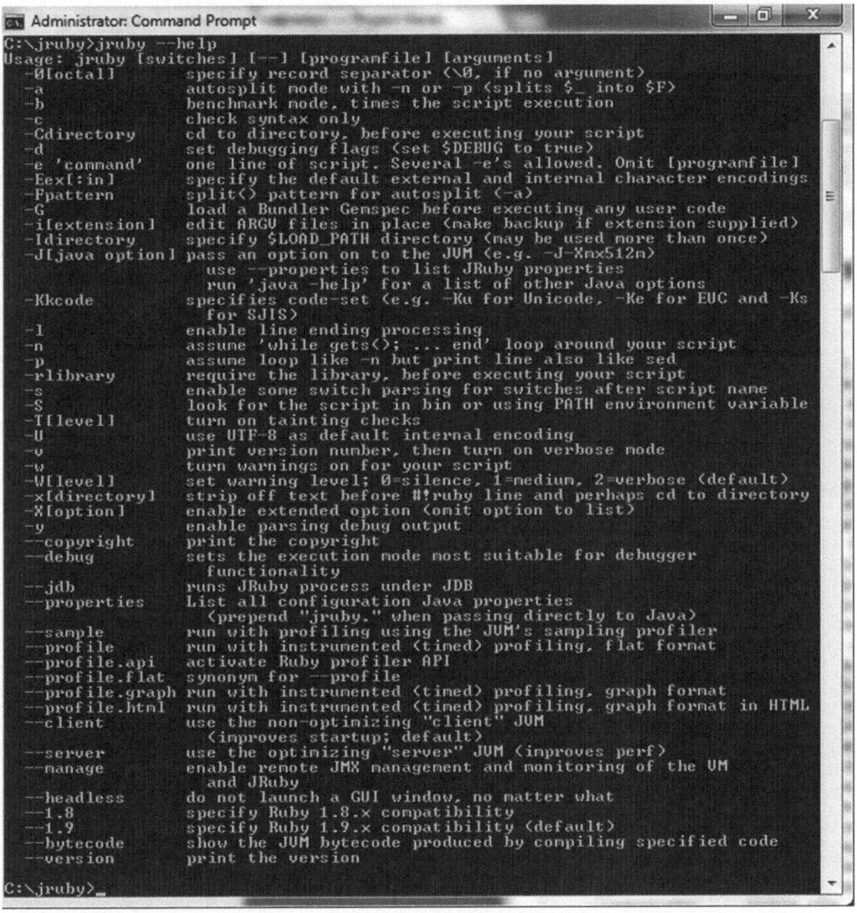

Administrator: Command Prompt
C:\jruby>jruby --help
Usage: jruby [switches] [--] [programfile] [arguments]
-0[octal] specify record separator (\0, if no argument)
-a autosplit mode with -n or -p (splits $_ into $F)
-b benchmark mode, times the script execution
-c check syntax only
-Cdirectory cd to directory, before executing your script
-d set debugging flags (set $DEBUG to true)
-e 'command' one line of script. Several -e's allowed. Omit [programfile]
-Eex[:in] specify the default external and internal character encodings
-Fpattern split() pattern for autosplit (-a)
-G load a Bundler Gemspec before executing any user code
-i[extension] edit ARGV files in place (make backup if extension supplied)
-Idirectory specify $LOAD_PATH directory (may be used more than once)
-J[java option] pass an option on to the JVM (e.g. -J-Xmx512m)
use --properties to list JRuby properties
run 'java -help' for a list of other Java options
-Kkcode specifies code-set (e.g. -Ku for Unicode, -Ke for EUC and -Ks
for SJIS)
-l enable line ending processing
-n assume 'while gets(); ... end' loop around your script
-p assume loop like -n but print line also like sed
-rlibrary require the library, before executing your script
-s enable some switch parsing for switches after script name
-S look for the script in bin or using PATH environment variable
-T[level] turn on tainting checks
-U use UTF-8 as default internal encoding
-v print version number, then turn on verbose mode
-w turn warnings on for your script
-W[level] set warning level; 0=silence, 1=medium, 2=verbose (default)
-x[directory] strip off text before #!ruby line and perhaps cd to directory
-X[option] enable extended option (omit option to list)
-y enable parsing debug output
--copyright print the copyright
--debug sets the execution mode most suitable for debugger
functionality
--jdb runs JRuby process under JDB
--properties List all configuration Java properties
(prepend "jruby." when passing directly to Java)
--sample run with profiling using the JVM's sampling profiler
--profile run with instrumented (timed) profiling, flat format
--profile.api activate Ruby profiler API
--profile.flat synonym for --profile
--profile.graph run with instrumented (timed) profiling, graph format
--profile.html run with instrumented (timed) profiling, graph format in HTML
--client use the non-optimizing "client" JVM
(improves startup; default)
--server use the optimizing "server" JVM (improves perf)
--manage enable remote JMX management and monitoring of the VM
and JRuby
--headless do not launch a GUI window, no matter what
--1.8 specify Ruby 1.8.x compatibility
--1.9 specify Ruby 1.9.x compatibility (default)
--bytecode show the JVM bytecode produced by compiling specified code
--version print the version
C:\jruby>_

Fig. 1.8 JRuby help

The JRuby version may be output with the `jruby -v` command. The interactive Ruby shell may be started with the following command.

```
>irb
```

Run a simple Ruby statement in irb.

```
irb>$a="Hello Jruby"
```

The output is shown in Fig. 1.7.

The usage of the `jruby` command may be listed with the `jruby -help` command as shown in Fig. 1.8.

In Chap. 2 we shall run a simple JRuby Script.

Chapter 2
Running a JRuby Script

In this chapter we shall run a simple JRuby script. JRuby script is just a Ruby script, Ruby 1.9 syntax is almost completely supported. Save the following JRuby script in a file (hello.rb).

```
class HelloWorld
      def hello()
            puts "Hello JRuby";
      end
end
a = HelloWorld.new
  a.hello
```

Add C:/jruby-1.7.0.RC2/lib/jruby.jar to CLASSPATH environment variable. From the directory containing the hello.rb compile the script using the Ahead-Of-Time (AOT) compiler with the following command.

```
>jrubyc hello.rb
```

The AOT compiler generates a .class file. Run the .class file just as you would run a Java class compiled from a .java file.

```
>java hello
```

The output from the jrubyc compiler and the java command is shown in Fig. 2.1.

The hello.rb script may also be run without AOT compilation using the jruby command.

```
>jruby hello.rb
```

The output is the same as running the script with AOT compilation and java command in sequence as shown in Fig. 2.2.

D. Vohra, *JRuby Rails Web Application Development*, SpringerBriefs in Computer Science, 7
DOI 10.1007/978-3-319-03934-3_2, © The Author(s) 2014

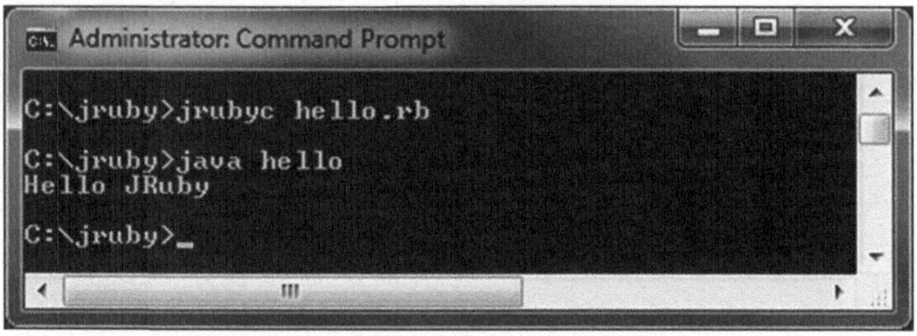

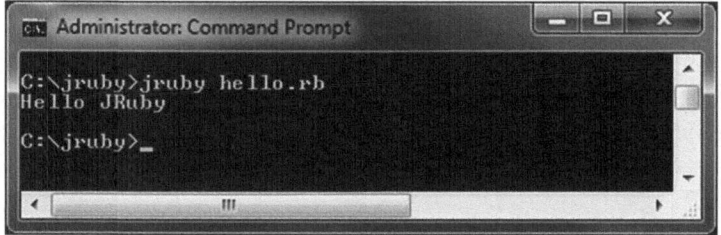

Fig. 2.1 Compiling and running a JRuby Script

Fig. 2.2 Running a JRuby Script with the jruby command

In the preceding example, The AOT compiler compiles the `hello.rb` Ruby script to a `.class` file, which is the runtime bytecode for the JVM. The `java` command runs the compiled `.class` file to generate an output. We did not use any Java code directly; the Ruby script was compiled into Java bytecode by the JRuby AOT compiler.

Next, we invoke Java™ from JRuby.

2.1 Invoking Java from JRuby

In this section we invoke a Java application from a JRuby script. A JRuby script is essentially a Ruby script not containing some of the not supported Ruby 1.9.x syntax. Create a Java class `CallJava.java` in package `com.example` as listed below.

```
package com.example;
public class CallJava {
String mName;
public CallJava() {
this("Default");
```

```
 }
public CallJava(String name) {
mName = name;
 }
public void hello() {
  System.out.println("Hello from "+mName);
  }
  public static void main(String []args) {
  System.out.println("Called main");
  }
  }
```

Next, compile the `CallJava.java` source code file using the `javac` command.

```
>javac CallJava.java
```

Having created and compiled a Java class, next we invoke the class from a JRuby script. Create a JRuby script `call_java_from_jruby.rb`. Java may be called from JRuby by including the `require "java"` directive. Java classes are imported using `java_import`. The `call_java_from_jruby.rb` creates a `java.util.TreeSet` object, adds elements to the set, and subsequently outputs the elements. The JRuby script also creates an instance of the `CallJava` class and invokes its `hello` method. The `call_java_from_jruby.rb` script is listed below.

```
require "java"
java_import "java.util.TreeSet"
java_import "com.example.CallJava"
puts "Hello from jruby"
set = TreeSet.new
set.add "call"
set.add "Java"
set.add "from"
set.add "JRuby"
set.each { |v| puts "value: #{v}" }
cj = CallJava.new
cj.hello
```

Run the JRuby script `call_java_from_jruby.rb`, which invokes the `CallJava` Java class, with the following command.

```
>jruby call_java_from_jruby.rb
```

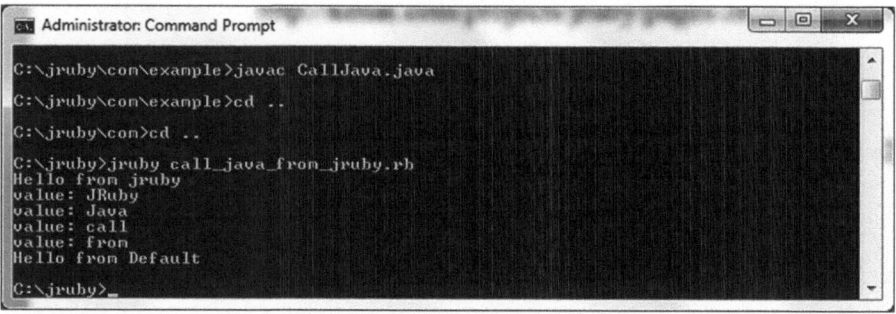

Fig. 2.3   Output from invoking Java from a JRuby Script

The output is shown in Fig. 2.3.

In the next chapter we shall get started with developing a Rails application with JRuby.

Chapter 3
Setting the Environment for a JRuby Web Application

JRuby may be used to develop a web application that may be run from any Java™ EE compliant application server. JRuby supports most relational databases. We develop a Rails application with JRuby and deploy and run the JRuby application with JBoss™ application server 7 and Oracle™ WebLogic Server. We use Oracle™ Database 11g XE as the database with WebLogicServer, and MySQL™ database as the database with JBoss application server 7. We need to install and configure the following software:

- Install JBoss Application Server 7
- Install MySQL Database
- Install Oracle WebLogic Server
- Install Oracle Database 11g XE
- Add Oracle database and MySQL database JDBC driver JARs to classpath
- Create a WebLogic Server domain

First, download the install the following software; the latest versions of the software could be different than those listed in this chapter.

1. Download the `OracleXE112_Win32.zip` file for Oracle Database 11g XE from `http://www.oracle.com/technetwork/products/express-edition/downloads/index.html`. Extract the file to a directory. Double-click on the `DISK1/setup.exe` file to install Oracle Database 11g XE.
2. Download the `wls1211_win32.exe` program for WebLogic Server 12c from `http://www.oracle.com/technetwork/middleware/weblogic/downloads/wls-main-097127.html`. Double-click on the `.exe` file to install WebLogic Server.
3. Download the MySQL Database Windows Installer `mysql-installer-community-5.6.10.1.exe` from `http://dev.mysql.com/downloads/installer/`. Double-click on the `.exe` file to start the MySQL Installer and install and configure MySQL Database.

D. Vohra, *JRuby Rails Web Application Development*, SpringerBriefs in Computer Science, DOI 10.1007/978-3-319-03934-3_3, © The Author(s) 2014

4. Download the `jboss-as-7.1.1.Final.zip` file from `http://www.jboss.org/jbossas/downloads/` and extract the file to a directory.

Add the Oracle JDBC driver JAR file `C:\Oracle\Middleware\wlserver_12.1\server\lib\ojdbc6.jar` to `CLASSPATH`. For MySQL database add the MySQL JDBC JAR file `C:\Program Files\MySQL\Connector J 5.1.23\mysql-connector-java-5.1.23-bin.jar` to `CLASSPATH`.

3.1 Creating a Oracle WebLogic Server Domain

We need to create a WebLogic Server domain. Start the Configuration Wizard. Select **Create a new WebLogic domain** and click on **Next**. For **Domain Source** select **Generate a domain configured automatically to support the following products**, which has the **Basic WebLogic Server domain 12.1.1.0** pre-selected. Click on **Next**. In **Specify Domain Name and Location** specify **Domain name** as **base_domain**, and **Domain location** as **C:\Oracle\Middleware\user_projects\ domains**. Click on **Next**. In **Configure Administration User Name and Password** specify a **Name** and **User password**. Click on **Next**. In **Configure Server Start Mode and JDK** select **Other JDK** and select the **jdk1.7.0_05**, and click on **Next**. In **Select Optional Configuration** click on **Next**. In **Configuration Summary** click on **Create**. The **base_domain** gets created. Click on **Done**.

We have installed Oracle WebLogic Server and JBoss application server 7 as we shall be deploying and running the JRuby web application on WebLogic Server and JBoss application server. We installed Java 7 as Java 6 or later is required for JRuby; Java 5 is not supported by JRuby 1.7. We installed Oracle Database 11g XE and MySQL as the databases for the Rails web application and also to store Rails sessions.

In Chap. 4 we create a JRuby Rails application.

Chapter 4
Creating a JRuby Rails Application

Rails is a Web application framework for developing database based Web applications using the Model-View-Controller (MVC) design pattern. The View layer consists of templates for user interface. The Model layer provides the business logic and the Controller layer takes incoming requests and returns a response. In this chapter we shall create a JRuby on Rails application for which:

- Install Rails
- Install ActiveRecord JDBC Adapter
- Install JRuby OpenSSL Gem
- Create a new Rails application

4.1 Installing Rails

Download the gem file `rails-3.1.8.gem` (http://rubygems.org/gems/rails/versions). Copy the Rails gem file to a directory, `c:/jruby`. From the `c:/jruby` directory run the following command.

```
jruby -S gem install rails
```

The `activesupport`, `actionpack`, `activerecord`, `activeresource`, and `actionmailer` gems, which constitute rails, get installed as shown in Fig. 4.1. The `actionpack` package is for the View and Controller layers and the `activerecord` package is for the Model layer.

D. Vohra, *JRuby Rails Web Application Development*, SpringerBriefs in Computer Science, 13
DOI 10.1007/978-3-319-03934-3_4, © The Author(s) 2014

```
Administrator: Command Prompt                                    _  □  X

C:\jruby>jruby -S gem install rails
Fetching: activesupport-3.1.8.gem (100%)
Fetching: actionpack-3.1.8.gem (100%)
Fetching: activerecord-3.1.8.gem (100%)
Fetching: activeresource-3.1.8.gem (100%)
Fetching: actionmailer-3.1.8.gem (100%)
Successfully installed activesupport-3.1.8
Successfully installed actionpack-3.1.8
Successfully installed activerecord-3.1.8
Successfully installed activeresource-3.1.8
Successfully installed actionmailer-3.1.8
Successfully installed rails-3.1.8
6 gems installed

C:\jruby>
```

Fig. 4.1 Installing Rails

4.2   Installing ActiveRecord JDBC Adapter

Install the `activerecord-jdbc-adapter` gem, which is required to use JRuby
with any JDBC supporting relational database such as the Oracle™ Database, with
the following command.

```
jruby -S gem install activerecord-jdbc-adapter
```

4.3   Installing JRuby OpenSSL Gem

Install the JRuby-OpenSSL gem with the following command.

```
jruby -S gem install jruby-openssl
```

The gems including dependencies get installed as shown in Fig. 4.2.
For MySQL™ database install the activerecord-`jdbcmysql-adapter` with the
following command.

```
gem install activerecord-jdbcmysql-adapter
```

The MySQLActiveRecord JDBC adapter gets installed as shown in Fig. 4.3.

4.4   Creating a Rails Application

Create a Rails application called `catalogs` with the following command; specify
the `database` option as `oracle`.

```
jruby -S rails new catalogs --database=oracle
```

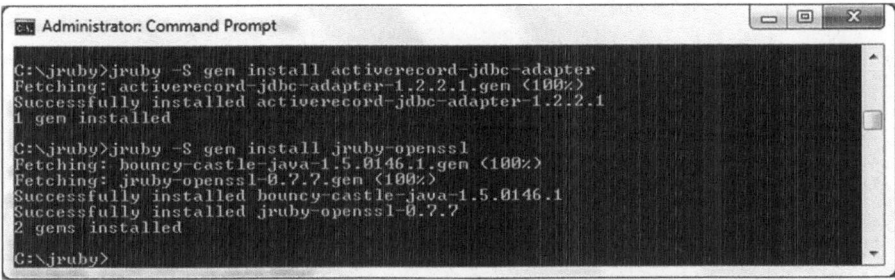

Fig. 4.2 Installing the ActiveRecord-JDBC-Adapter and JRuby-OpenSSL Gems

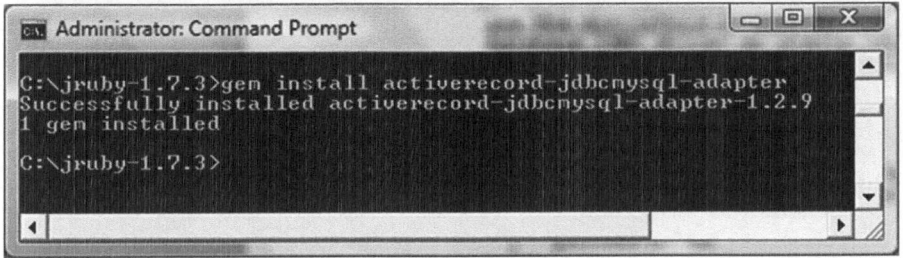

Fig. 4.3 Installing the MySQL ActiveRecord JDBC Adapter gem

The Rails application `catalogs` including the application artifacts get created as shown in Fig. 4.4.

The directory structure of the `catalogs` application is shown in Fig. 4.5.

If MySQL database is used, run the following command instead of the previous command to create a Rails application.

```
jruby -S rails new catalogs --database=mysql
```

The output from the command with MySQL database as shown in Fig. 4.6 is similar to the Oracle database output.

We shall be using MySQL database and Oracle database with Rails `ActiveRecord` component. To be able to use the `ActiveRecord` component with JRuby we installed a database adapter, the `activerecord-jdbc-adapter`, which supports any JDBC-compliant database. Some other database specific adapters are also available. We installed the JRuby-OpenSSL gem, which emulates the Ruby OpenSSL native library. We created a Rails application using the syntax to create a new Rails application, which is as follows.

```
jruby -S rails new APP_PATH <options>
```

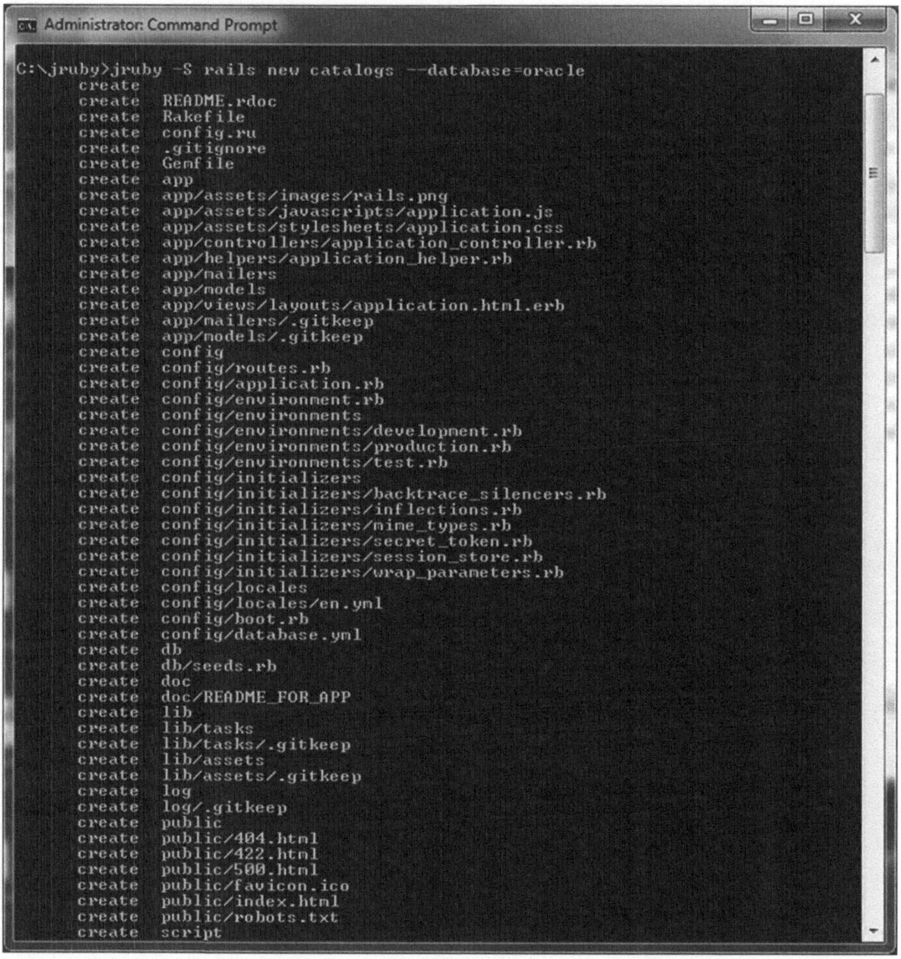

Fig. 4.4 Creating a Rails application

The Rails application is a MVC (Model-View-Controller) application. The `app/` `controllers/application_controller` script specifies the application controller class `ApplicationController`, which extends the `ActionController::Base` class.

```
class ApplicationController < ActionController::Base
end
```

Rails 3.1 introduced the "asset pipeline" to integrate the Sprockets gem and provide a built-in framework to pre-process, concatenate, and compress CSS and JavaScript resources (assets). The default layout for a Rails application is defined in the `app/views/layouts/application.html.erb` script. If the "Asset

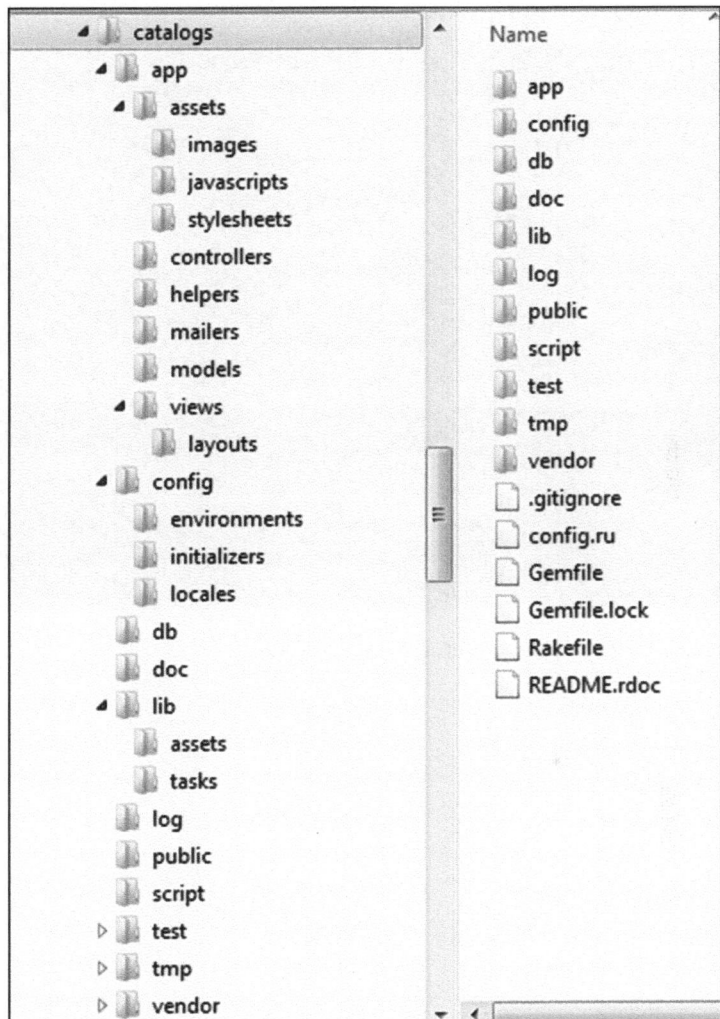

Fig. 4.5 The directory structure of the Rails application

Pipeline" is enabled, which it is by default, the `stylesheet_link_tag` is a helper tag that provides a mechanism to link to CSS files in the `app/assets/ stylesheets`, `lib/assets/stylesheets` and `vendor/assets/ stylesheets` directories. The tag returns a `<link>` tag, which is processed by the Sprockets gem. By default, a new Rails application consists of an `app/assets/ stylesheets/application.css` file. To access the JavaScript assets, the Sprockets concatenates and links the JavaScript assets specified in the `javascript_include_tag` tag. The `application.html.erb` layout file with the Sprockets supported link tags is listed below.

```
Administrator: Command Prompt

C:\jruby-1.7.3>jruby -S rails new catalogs --database=mysql
      create
      create   README
      create   Rakefile
      create   config.ru
      create   .gitignore
      create   Gemfile
      create   app
      create   app/assets/images/rails.png
      create   app/assets/javascripts/application.js
      create   app/assets/stylesheets/application.css
      create   app/controllers/application_controller.rb
      create   app/helpers/application_helper.rb
      create   app/mailers
      create   app/models
      create   app/views/layouts/application.html.erb
      create   app/mailers/.gitkeep
      create   app/models/.gitkeep
      create   config
      create   config/routes.rb
      create   config/application.rb
      create   config/environment.rb
      create   config/environments
      create   config/environments/development.rb
      create   config/environments/production.rb
      create   config/environments/test.rb
      create   config/initializers
      create   config/initializers/backtrace_silencers.rb
      create   config/initializers/inflections.rb
```

Fig. 4.6 Creating a Rails application using MySQL database

```
<!DOCTYPE html>
<html>
<head>
  <title>Catalogs</title>
  <%= stylesheet_link_tag    "application" %>
<%= javascript_include_tag "application" %>
 <%= csrf_meta_tags %>
</head>
<body>
    <%= yield %>
</body>
</html>
```

In Chap. 5 we configure the databases for a Rails web application.

Chapter 5
Configuring Databases for a JRuby Web Application

Configuring databases implies configuring database parameters in a configuration file (`database.yml`) so that the JRuby on Rails application may access a database. For Oracle™ database, to use ActiveRecord JDBC configure the `activerecord-jdbc-adapter` adapter in the `database.yml`. For Oracle database, configure Oracle Database in two environment modes: `development` and `production`. The Oracle™ WebLogic Server, even when started in development mode, requires the production database to be configured in `database.yml`. For running rake tasks such as `db:migrate` and `db:create` the development database is required. At the least the `url` and `driver` parameters are required to configured. For MySQL™ database configure the `activerecord-jdbcmysql-adapter` adapter. The parameters for MySQL database are different than for Oracle database.

When we create a Rails application a `config/database.yml` file gets created.

5.1 Configuring Oracle Database in Rails Application

Next, configure the `production` environment database for Oracle database in `database.yml`. Set the `adapter` parameter to `jdbc` for Oracle Database to use the ActiveRecord adapter for JDBC and JRuby. Specify the Oracle Database JDBC driver using the `driver` parameter to `oracle.jdbc.OracleDriver`. Specify the connection `url` parameter as `jdbc:oracle:thin:@localhost:1521:XE`. Also specify the `username` and `password` as listed below.

```
production:
    adapter: jdbc
    driver: oracle.jdbc.OracleDriver
    url: jdbc:oracle:thin:@localhost:1521:XE
    username: OE
    password: OE
```

D. Vohra, *JRuby Rails Web Application Development*, SpringerBriefs in Computer Science, 19
DOI 10.1007/978-3-319-03934-3_5, © The Author(s) 2014

Similarly, configure the `development` environment database for Oracle database in `database.yml` as listed below. All the configuration parameters are the same as for the production environment.

```
development:
    adapter: jdbc
    driver: oracle.jdbc.OracleDriver
    url: jdbc:oracle:thin:@localhost:1521:XE
    username: OE
    password: OE
```

5.2   Configuring MySQL Database in Rails Application

If using MySQL database configure the `database.yml` for MySQL database. Set the `adapter` parameter to `mysql` and database to `test` in the connection `url`. Set `driver` to `com.mysql.jdbc.Driver`.

```
development:
    adapter: mysql
    url: "jdbc:mysql://localhost:3306/test"
    driver: com.mysql.jdbc.Driver
    username: root
    password: mysql

production:
    adapter: mysql
    url: "jdbc:mysql://localhost:3306/test"
    driver: com.mysql.jdbc.Driver
    username: root
    password: mysql
```

The `production` section specifies the production environment database and the `development` section specifies the development environment database. The database adapter name is specified using the `adapter` parameter. The `driver` parameter specifies the JDBC driver to be used. The `url` parameter specifies the connection url to be used. The `username` parameter specifies the user name and `password` parameter specifies the password.

In Chap. 6 we create scaffolding for a Rails application.

Chapter 6
Creating Scaffolding for a JRuby Rails Application

Rails scaffolding consists of the basic components that represent the model, view and controller layers of a Rails application including support for the CRUD (Create, Read, Update, and Delete) operations.

Having created a Rails application as discussed in Chap. 4 and having configured the databases in Chap. 5, in this chapter we create the scaffolding for the Rails application.

6.1 Generating Scaffolding

Generate a scaffold for the `catalog` resource with properties `journal` of type `string`, publisher of type `string`, `edition` of type `string`, and `description` of type `text`, using the `rails generate scaffold` command. Change directory (`cd`) to the catalogs directory before running the command.

```
catalogs> rails generate scaffold catalog journal:string
publisher:string edition:string description:text
```

A set of files and folders for a model, database migrations, controller, and views gets generated as shown in Fig. 6.1.

6.2 The Controller Script

The `app/controllers/catalog_controllers` script specifies the controller class `CatalogsController`, which extends the `ApplicationController`. The controller class has methods `index`, `show`, `new`, `edit`, `create`, `update`, and

D. Vohra, *JRuby Rails Web Application Development*, SpringerBriefs in Computer Science, 21
DOI 10.1007/978-3-319-03934-3_6, © The Author(s) 2014

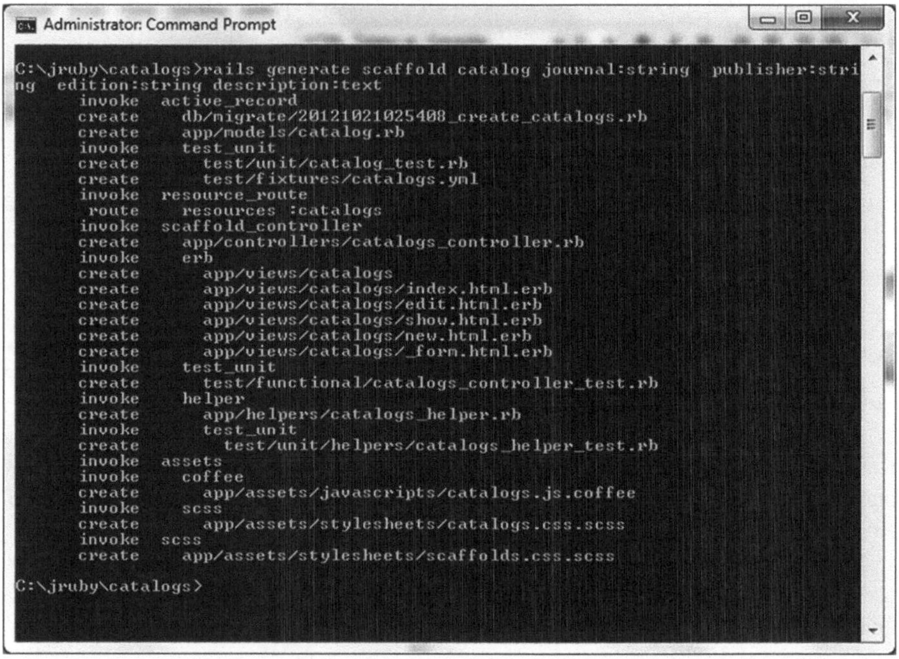

Fig. 6.1 Creating scaffolding for the Rails application catalogs

destroy to perform CRUD operations for a catalog entry. Replace the ':' with '=>'
for key/value pairs in a Ruby Hash, and prefix variables with ':'. For example,
replace:

```
format.html { redirect_to @journal, notice: 'Journal was suc-
cessfully created.' }
```

with:

```
format.html { redirect_to @journal, :notice => 'Journal was
successfully created.' }
```

The controller script, which may be customized, is listed below.

```
class CatalogsController < ApplicationController
    # GET /catalogs
    # GET /catalogs.json
    def index
      @catalogs = Catalog.all
      respond_to do |format|
        format.html # index.html.erb
        format.json { render json => @catalogs }
      end
    end
    # GET /catalogs/1
```

```ruby
  # GET /catalogs/1.json
  def show
    @catalog = Catalog.find(params[:id])
    respond_to do |format|
      format.html # show.html.erb
      format.json { render json => @catalog }
    end
  end
  # GET /catalogs/new
  # GET /catalogs/new.json
  def new
    @catalog = Catalog.new
    respond_to do |format|
      format.html # new.html.erb
      format.json { render json => @catalog }
    end
  end
  # GET /catalogs/1/edit
  def edit
    @catalog = Catalog.find(params[:id])
  end
  # POST /catalogs
  # POST /catalogs.json
  def create
    @catalog = Catalog.new(params[:catalog])
    respond_to do |format|
      if @catalog.save
          format.html { redirect_to @catalog, :notice =>
'Catalog was successfully created.' }
          format.json { render json => @catalog, status =>
:created, location => @catalog }
        else
          format.html { render action => "new" }
          format.json { render json => @catalog.errors, status
=> :unprocessable_entity }
        end
end
    end
  end
  # PUT /catalogs/1
  # PUT /catalogs/1.json
  def update
    @catalog = Catalog.find(params[:id])
    respond_to do |format|
      if @catalog.update_attributes(params[:catalog])
          format.html { redirect_to @catalog, :notice =>
'Catalog was successfully updated.' }
      format.json { head :ok }
        else
```

```
        format.html { render action => "edit" }
        format.json { render json => @catalog.errors, status
=> :unprocessable_entity }
      end
    end
  end
  # DELETE /catalogs/1
  # DELETE /catalogs/1.json
  def destroy
    @catalog = Catalog.find(params[:id])
    @catalog.destroy
    respond_to do |format|
      format.html { redirect_to catalogs_url }
      format.json { head :ok }
    end
  end
end
```

6.3   The Model Script

The model script `app/models/catalog.rb` consists of class `Catalog`, which extends the `ActiveRecord::Base` class.

```
class Catalog < ActiveRecord::Base
```

6.4   The View Scripts

To create, update, and view model data `index.html.erb`, `new.html.erb`, `show.html.erb`, `edit.html.erb`, and `_form.html.erb` get created in the `app/views/catalogs` folder. Replace ':' in key/value pairs with '=>' and prefix variable names with ':' in `index.html.erb`. For example, replace:

```
<%= link_to 'Destroy', journal, confirm: 'Are you sure?',
method: :delete %>
```

with:

```
<%= link_to 'Destroy', journal, :confirm => 'Are you sure?',
:method => :delete %>
```

The `app/views/catalogs/index.html.erb` script iterates over the catalog entries and displays them in a table format. Links are provided to create a new catalog entry, edit a catalog, show and delete a catalog. The `index.html.erb` is listed below.

```
<h1>Listing catalogs</h1>
<table>
    <tr>
      <th>Journal</th>
      <th>Publisher</th>
      <th>Edition</th>
      <th>Description</th>
      <th></th>
      <th></th>
      <th></th>
    </tr>
<% @catalogs.each do |catalog| %>
    <tr>
      <td><%= catalog.journal %></td>
      <td><%= catalog.publisher %></td>
      <td><%= catalog.edition %></td>
      <td><%= catalog.description %></td>
      <td><%= link_to 'Show', catalog %></td>
      <td><%= link_to 'Edit', edit_catalog_path(catalog)
%></td>
      <td><%= link_to 'Destroy', catalog, :confirm =>
'Are you sure?', :method => :delete %></td>
    </tr>
<% end %>
</table>
<br />
<%= link_to 'New Catalog', new_catalog_path %>
```

The new.html.erb renders a form to create a new catalog.

```
<h1>New catalog</h1>
<%= render 'form' %>
<%= link_to 'Back', catalogs_path %>
```

The show.html.erb displays a catalog with its properties journal, publisher, edition, and description.

```
<p id="notice"><%= :notice %></p>
<p>
    <b>Journal:</b>
    <%= @catalog.journal %>
</p>
<p>
    <b>Publisher:</b>
    <%= @catalog.publisher %>
</p>
<p>
    <b>Edition:</b>
    <%= @catalog.edition %>
</p>
<p>
```

```
    <b>Description:</b>
    <%= @catalog.description %>
</p>
<%= link_to 'Edit', edit_catalog_path(@catalog) %> |
<%= link_to 'Back', catalogs_path %>
```

The `edit.html.erb` displays a form to edit a catalog entry.

```
<h1>Editing catalog</h1>
<%= render 'form' %>
<%= link_to 'Show', @catalog %> |
<%= link_to 'Back', catalogs_path %>
```

The `_form.html.erb` consists of a form with labels and fields for `journal`, `publisher`, `edition`, and `description` and a submit button.

```
    <%= form_for(@catalog) do |f| %>
      <% if @catalog.errors.any? %>
        <div id="error_explanation">
          <h2><%= pluralize(@catalog.errors.count, "error") %>
prohibited this catalog from being saved:</h2>
          <ul>
          <% @catalog.errors.full_messages.each do |msg| %>
            <li><%= msg %></li>
          <% end %>
          </ul>
        </div>
      <% end %>
      <div class="field">
        <%= f.label :journal %><br />
        <%= f.text_field :journal %>
      </div>
      <div class="field">
        <%= f.label :publisher %><br />
        <%= f.text_field :publisher %>
      </div>
      <div class="field">
        <%= f.label :edition %><br />
        <%= f.text_field :edition %>
      </div>
      <div class="field">
        <%= f.label :description %><br />
        <%= f.text_area :description %>
      </div>
      <div class="actions">
        <%= f.submit %>
      </div>
    <% end %>
```

Assets for the scaffolding get generated in the `app/assets/javascripts` and `app/assets/stylesheets` directories.

Chapter 7
Creating Database Tables by Running Migrations

We shall need a database to store data for the JRuby on Rails application. Next, create the database table. We shall use migrations to create a database table in Oracle™ database or MySQL™ database. Migrations are Ruby classes used to create and update database tables.

The Oracle database service `OracleServiceXE` and listener `OracleXETNS-Listener` must be running before creating the database table. For MySQL database the MySQL database service must be running. The `development` database is required to be configured in `database.yml`. When the scaffolding is created in Chap. 6 a migration script to create a database table `catalogs` also gets created in the `db/migrate` directory.

7.1 Creating the Migration Script

If the migration script in the `db/migrate` directory is not created, or was deleted, create a migration script for database table for the Rails application with the following command.

```
jruby -S rake db:create:all
```

Migration script `db/migrate/ 20121021173759_create_catalogs.rb` gets created, and is listed.

```
class CreateCatalogs < ActiveRecord::Migration
  def change
    create_table :catalogs do |t|
      t.string :journal
      t.string :publisher
      t.string :edition
      t.text :description
      t.timestamps
```

D. Vohra, *JRuby Rails Web Application Development*, SpringerBriefs in Computer Science,   27
DOI 10.1007/978-3-319-03934-3_7, © The Author(s) 2014

```
      end
   end
end
```

The migration script has a timestamp in its name so that migrations are run in the order created.

7.2   Running the Migration Script

Next, run the migration script with the following command.

```
jruby -S rake db:migrate
```

The rake db:migrate command creates the catalogs table and the catalogs_seq sequence for Oracle database as shown in Fig. 7.1. The sequence is required as Oracle database does not support auto-increment of primary key ids.

The structure of the CATALOGS table in Oracle database is shown in Fig. 7.2. The DESCRIPTION column is of type CLOB. The CREATED_AT and UPDATED_AT timestamp columns of type DATE also get created.

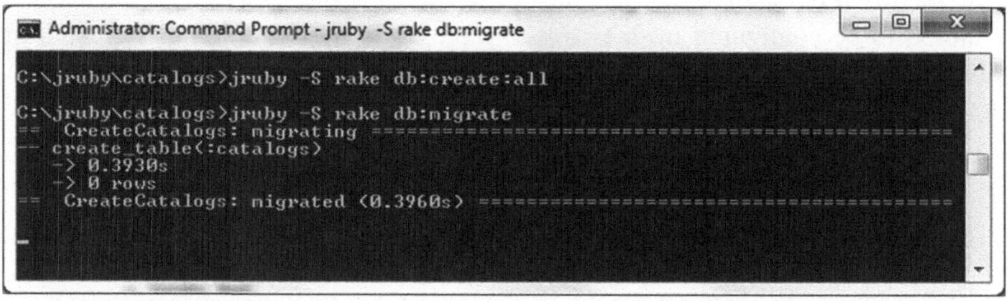

Fig. 7.1 Running migrations to create Oracle database table catalogs

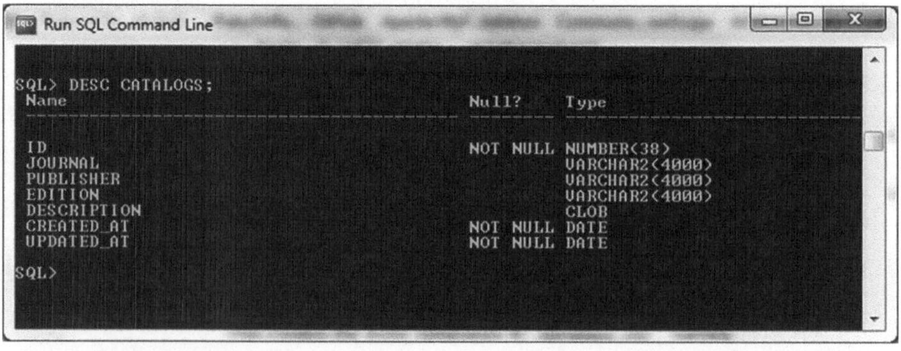

Fig. 7.2 The structure of the catalogs database table

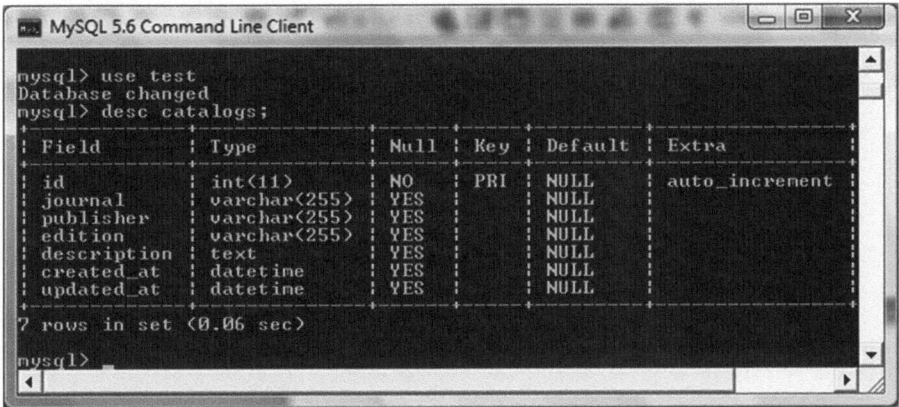

Fig. 7.3 Structure of catalogs database table in MySQL database

As MySQL database supports autoincrement of primary key values, a sequence is not created with MySQL database. The structure of the MySQL database table `catalogs` is shown in Fig. 7.3.

In Chap. 8 we precompile the Rails application "assets".

Chapter 8
Precompiling CSS and JavaScript Assets

Rails 3.1 introduced the Sprockets based assets pipeline to precompile and merge all the different stylesheets into one and merge all the JavaScripts into one for the deployed web application. Precompiling and merging assets reduces the time to load web pages as fewer requests to assets are required. Also, if compression is used for assets compilation the amount of data transfer is reduced. Sprockets makes use of the manifest files `app/assets/javascripts/application.js` and `app/assets/stylesheets/application.css`, which contain directives, to select resources to merge and serve as static assets by the web server. By default, the `application.js` consists of `require` directives for the `jquery.js` and `jquery_ujs.js` that are in the Sprockets search path, and the `require_tree` directive to recursively include all JavaScript files in the specified directory, which is the '.' directory (current directory). To include JavaScript files without recursion use the `require_directory` directive.

```
//= require jquery
//= require jquery_ujs
//= require_tree .
```

Manifest file `application.css` and stylesheets `catalogs.css.scss` and `scaffolds.css.scss` get generated in the `app/assets/stylesheets` directory. The `require_self` directive in the Manifest file includes the CSS in the manifest file and the `require_tree` directive is used to recursively include all stylesheets in the specified directory.

```
/*
 *
 *= require_self
 *= require_tree .
*/
```

D. Vohra, *JRuby Rails Web Application Development*, SpringerBriefs in Computer Science, 31
DOI 10.1007/978-3-319-03934-3_8, © The Author(s) 2014

We created a Rails application in Chap. 4 and created scaffolding for the Rails application in Chap. 6. Before deploying the Rails application to Oracle™ WebLogic Server or JBoss™ application server we need to precompile the assets. It is recommended to precompile assets using the rake task.

8.1 Precompiling Assets

Before, we precompile, we need to set the following option in config/environments/production.rb.

```
config.assets.digest = false
```

Run the rake task to precompile assets.

```
rake assets:precompile
```

The assets get precompiled as shown in the output from the rake command in Fig. 8.1.

By default the assets get compiled into the public/assets folder, and shown in Fig. 8.2.

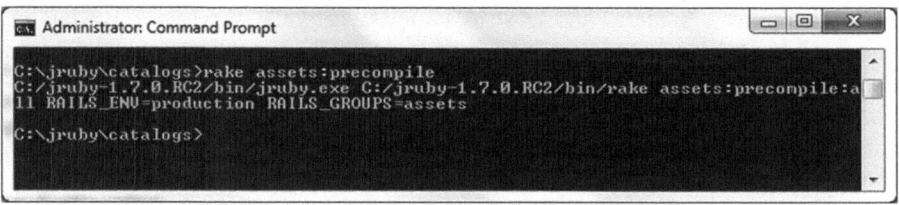

Fig. 8.1 Precompiling assets

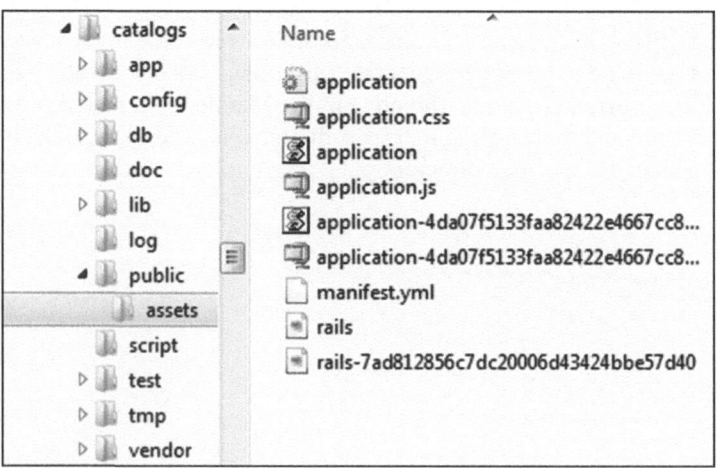

Fig. 8.2 Compiled assets

After precompiling assets, set the configuration option for fingerprinting, which is used in production to name files based on file contents to differentiate different versions of a file, to `true` in `production.rb`.

```
config.assets.digest = true
```

The rake command to precompile assets compiles and merges the CSS stylesheets and JavaScript files. Live compilation is also supported with the following setting in `\catalogs\config\environments\production.rb`.

```
config.assets.compile = true
```

But, live compilation's performance is not reliable and was tested and found not to make JavaScripts available at runtime.

In Chap. 9 we enable flash to be able to store messages.

Chapter 9
Enabling Flash

A Rails application generates messages indicating the outcome of some action or an error. Rails provides the Flash hash to store the messages in the session and make them available in another request, the next request by default. As the flash messages are stored in the session the Rails sessions need to be enabled. Rails sessions are configured in the `config/initializers/session_store.rb` file. The `session_store.rb` file recommends to use the database for sessions instead of the cookie-based default.

We shall use the Oracle™ Database or MySQL™ database to store sessions for which we need to create a `sessions` table. The Oracle database service and listener must be running. For MySQL database the MySQL service must be running. The `development` environment database is required to be configured in `database.yml` to create the `sessions` table.

9.1 Creating the Sessions Database Table

Run the following rake command to create the migration script for the `sessions` table.

```
rake db:sessions:create
```

Next, run the migration script to create a `sessions` table using the following command.

```
rake db:migrate
```

Modify `config/initializers/session_store.rb` file to use the database for sessions. Only the following declaration should be uncommented.

```
Catalogs::Application.config.session_store
:active_record_store
```

D. Vohra, *JRuby Rails Web Application Development*, SpringerBriefs in Computer Science, DOI 10.1007/978-3-319-03934-3_9, © The Author(s) 2014

To add an indicator for a flash message modify the layout file `apps/views/layouts/application.html.erb` to add the following statements.

```
<% if flash[:notice] %>
      <p class="notice"><%= flash[:notice] %></p>
      <% end %>
```

The following migration script `db/migrate/20121026010913_add_sessions_table.rb` gets created with the `rake  db:sessions:create` command.

```
class AddSessionsTable < ActiveRecord::Migration
   def up
      create_table :sessions do |t|
         t.string :session_id, :null => false
```

The output from the rake commands is shown in Fig. 9.1; a `sessions` table and indexes `session_id` and `updated_at` get created with the `rake  db: migrate` command.

In Chap. 10 we package the JRuby Rails application to a Web application.

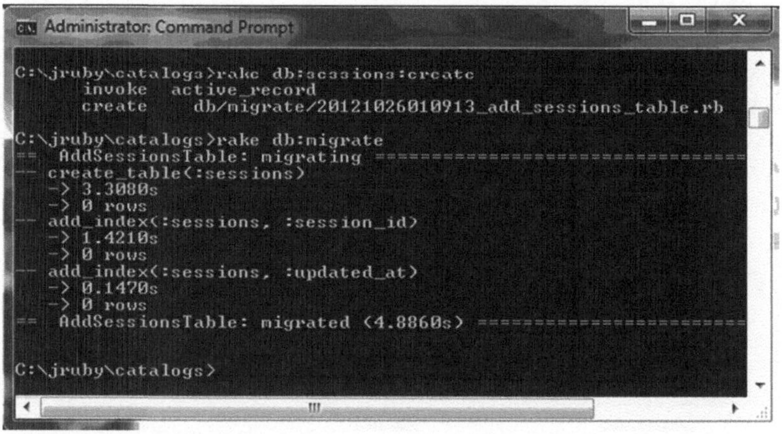

Fig. 9.1 Creating sessions table

Chapter 10
Packaging the JRuby Application as a Java™ EE Web Application

Having generated a Rails application we shall package the application into a WAR file using the warbler gem. A WAR archive is used to deploy a web application to a Java EE application server.

10.1 Installing Warbler

First, install the warbler gem using the following command from the JRuby installation directory.

```
jruby -S gem install warbler
```

Warbler gets installed as shown in the output in Fig. 10.1.

10.2 Configuring Warbler

If using Oracle™ WebLogic server we need to add some additional configuration. Because some WebLogic Server JAR file/s in the runtime classpath, such as the Joda time JAR, have classes that are also packaged into the WAR file generated by warbler and are the wrong version, we need to add a `weblogic.xml` file into the war file to indicate that the WAR packaged files in the `WEB-INF` directory be used instead of JAR files in the server runtime classpath. Add the following `weblogic.xml` file to the `catalogs/config` directory.

```
<weblogic-web-app xmlns="http://www.bea.com/ns/weblogic/
weblogic-web-app">
<container-descriptor>
    <!--
```

D. Vohra, *JRuby Rails Web Application Development*, SpringerBriefs in Computer Science, 37
DOI 10.1007/978-3-319-03934-3_10, © The Author(s) 2014

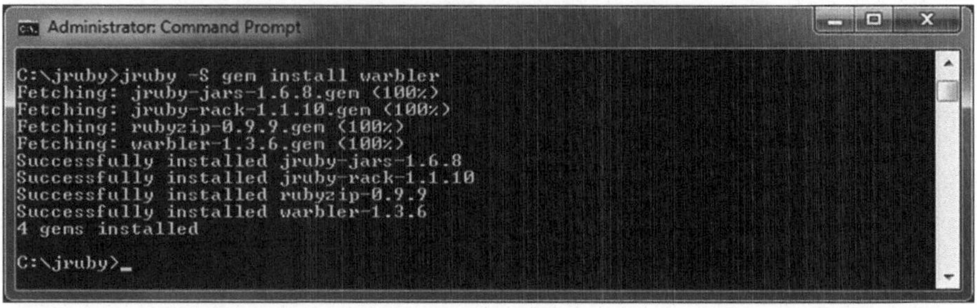

Fig. 10.1 Installing the warbler gem

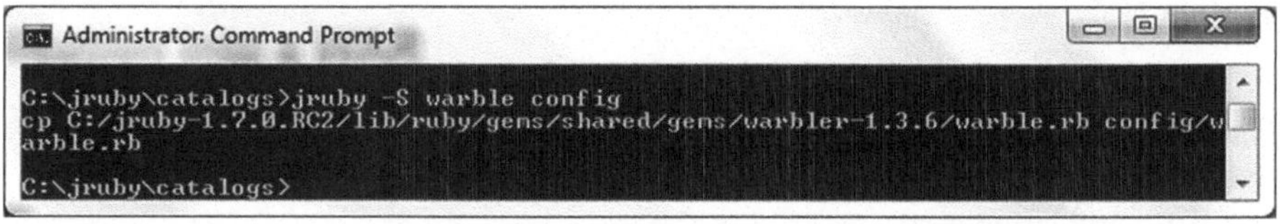

Fig. 10.2 Copying warble.rb to the config directory

```
    The following entry is necessary to prevent Weblogics
old version of
    the Joda time JAR (1.2.1) from taking precendence over
the much more
    recent version (1.6.0) included in JRuby. Without this
setting,
    Rails 3 will fail to start, due to the missing withYear
method on
    org.joda.time.DateTime.
-->
<prefer-web-inf-classes>true</prefer-web-inf-classes>
</container-descriptor>
</weblogic-web-app>
```

We need to configure the warbler so that the `config/weblogic.xml` file be included in the WAR file generated. Warbler provides the `warble.rb` file to customize the libraries, jars, and gems to include in the WAR file. Copy the `warble.rb` from the warbler gem directory to the `config` directory with the `jruby -S warble config` command run from the catalogs directory as shown in Fig. 10.2.

In the `/config/warble.rb` configure the files in addition to the `web.xml` to include in the `WEB-INF` directory using the `config.webinf_files` option.

```
Files  for  WEB-INF  directory  (next  to  web.xml).  This
contains
    # web.xml by default. If there  is  an  .erb-File it
will be processed
```

```
    # with webxml-config. You may want to exclude this
file via
    # config.excludes.
config.webinf_files += FileList["config/weblogic.xml"]
```

Also, configure the `activerecord-jdbc-adapter` gem in `warble.rb` in the `config.gems` declaration.

```
config.gems     += ["activerecord-jdbcmysql-adapter",
"activerecord-jdbc-adapter","jruby-openssl"]
```

10.3   Generating the Web Application

Next, we generate the web application WAR file from the JRuby Rails application using the warbler. Generate the WAR file using the following command from the `catalogs` directory.

```
>warble war
```

The `catalogs.war` gets generated as shown in Fig. 10.3.

The warbler gem is required to generate a WAR file from a JRuby Rails application. We installed and configured the warbler gem and subsequently generated the `catalogs.war` file. A developer is not required to have any knowledge about a web application or a WAR file structure to package the Rails application as a WAR file.

In Chap. 11 we deploy the `catalogs.war` Web application to WebLogic Server.

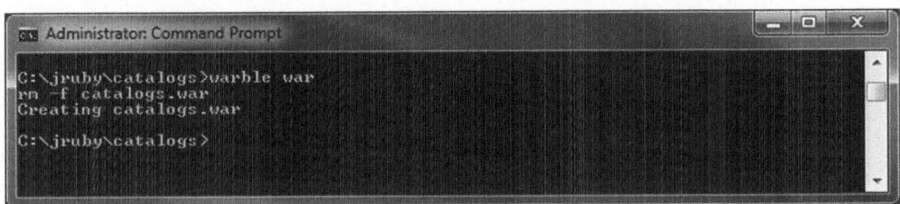

Fig. 10.3 Generating Web application WAR archive

Chapter 11
Running the Web Application in Oracle™ WebLogic Server

The catalogs.war may be deployed to Oracle WebLogic Server just as any other WAR file. In this chapter we deploy the web application to WebLogic server and subsequently run the web application in WebLogic server.

11.1 Deploying the Web Application

Start the WebLogic Server Admin Server for the base_domain. Login to the Admin Server Console and select base_domain|deployments. Click on **Install** to install the catalogs.war as shown in Fig. 11.1.

Select the **catalogs.war** from the **catalogs** application root folder and click on **Next** as shown in Fig. 11.2.

In **Choose targeting style** select **Install this deployment as an application** and click on Next. Select the default Optional Settings and click on Next. The Summary of the deployment gets displayed. Click on Finish. The catalogs.war application gets deployed to WebLogic Server. Click on Save to activate the changes and save the configuration settings as shown in Fig. 11.3.

Select the **Targets** tab; the **Admin Server** should be selected as the **target server**. Select **Deployments**, the **catalogs** application is shown as deployed as in Fig. 11.4.

The **Install Application Assistant** in Oracle WebLogic Server installs the **catalogs.war** to WebLogic Server from the Admin Server Console.

D. Vohra, *JRuby Rails Web Application Development*, SpringerBriefs in Computer Science,   41
DOI 10.1007/978-3-319-03934-3_11, © The Author(s) 2014

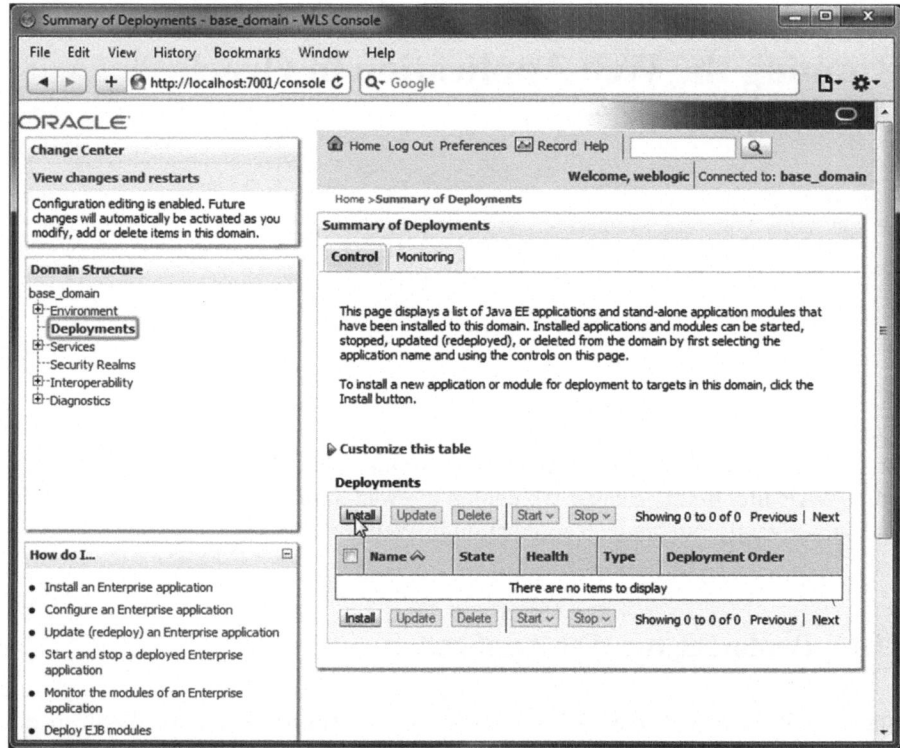

Fig. 11.1 Installing Web application to WebLogic Server using the Admin Console

11.2   Running the JRuby Web Application

We created a JRuby on Rails application. Subsequently, we packaged the Rails application to a WAR file using warbler. We deployed the `catalogs.war` file to WebLogic Server. Next, run the JRuby on Rails application deployed to WebLogic Server.

Invoke the URL `http://localhost:7001/catalogs/catalogs` in a browser. The `index.html.erb` gets displayed with a link to create a **New Catalog**. Click on **New Catalog** to create a new catalog as shown in Fig. 11.5.

In the **New catalog** page add values to catalog entry fields and click on **Create Catalog** as shown in Fig. 11.6.

A catalog entry gets created and a flash message gets displayed to indicate the same as shown in Fig. 11.7. Click on **Back** to navigate to the index page.

The new catalog entry is shown in the listing of catalogs. Click on **Show** to display a catalog entry as shown in Fig. 11.8.

The catalog entry gets displayed. Click on **Back** to navigate back to the index page. Click on **Edit** to edit a catalog entry. Modify the fields to be updated and click on **Update Catalog** as shown in Fig. 11.9.

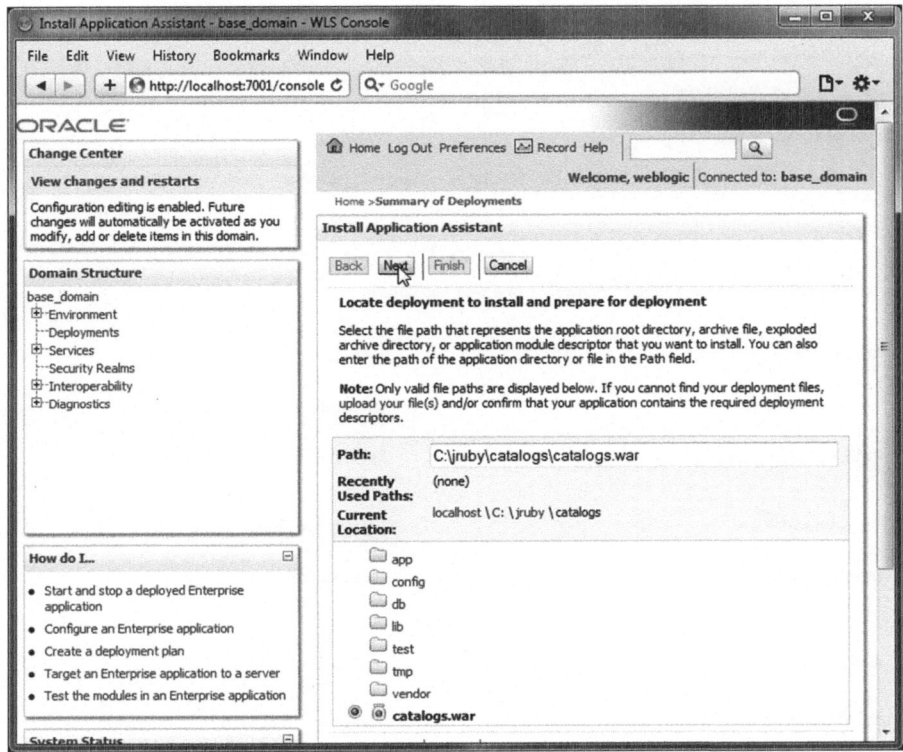

Fig. 11.2   Selecting the catalogs.war Web application

The catalog entry gets updated and a flash message gets displayed to indicate the same. Click on **Back** to navigate to the index page. The updated fields get listed in the catalog entry.

In Chap. 12 we run the same web application in JBoss™ 7 application server with MySQL™ database.

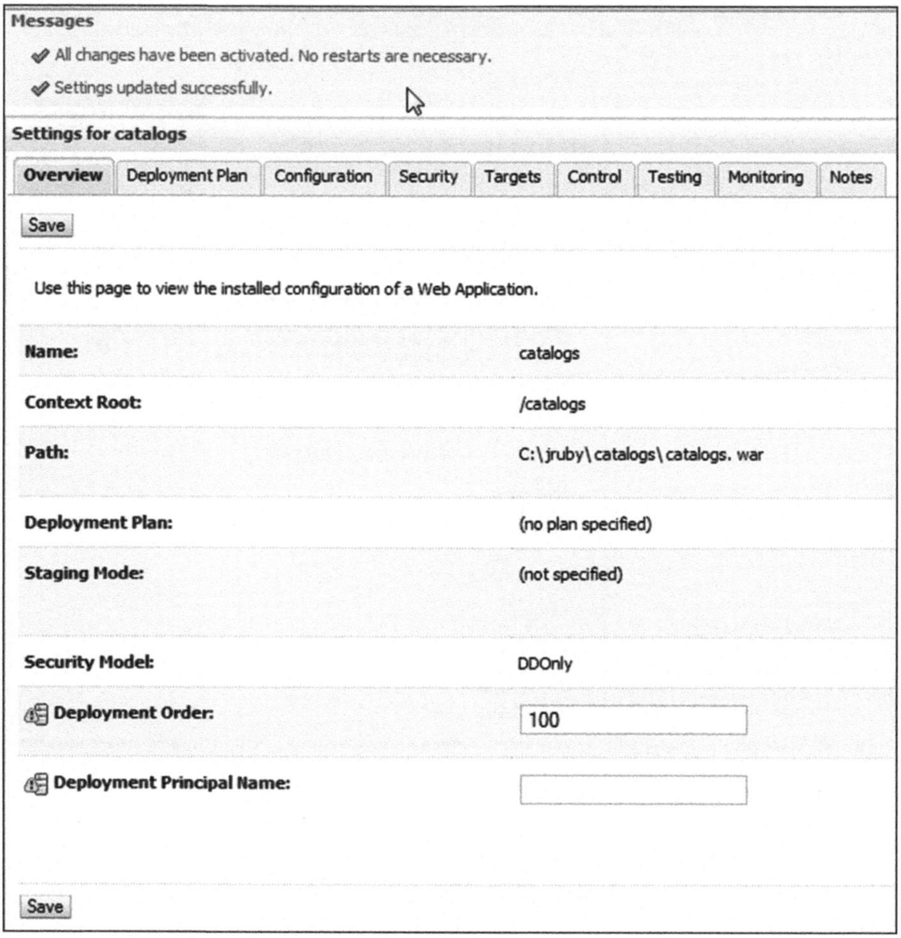

Messages

✔ All changes have been activated. No restarts are necessary.

✔ Settings updated successfully.

Settings for catalogs

Overview	Deployment Plan	Configuration	Security	Targets	Control	Testing	Monitoring	Notes

Save

Use this page to view the installed configuration of a Web Application.

Name:	catalogs
Context Root:	/catalogs
Path:	C:\jruby\catalogs\catalogs.war
Deployment Plan:	(no plan specified)
Staging Mode:	(not specified)
Security Model:	DDOnly
Deployment Order:	100
Deployment Principal Name:	

Save

Fig. 11.3 Saving configuration settings for catalogs.war

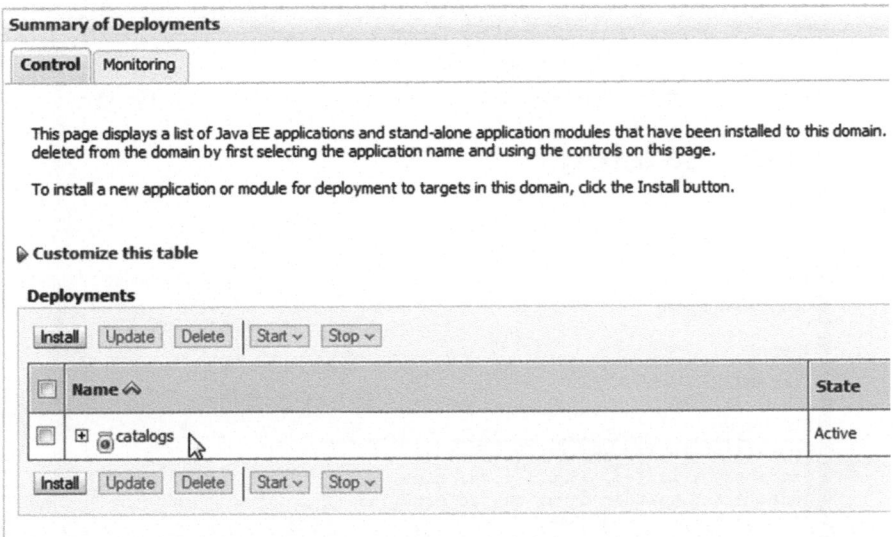

Fig. 11.4 The catalogs.war deployed to WebLogic Server as shown in the Admin Console

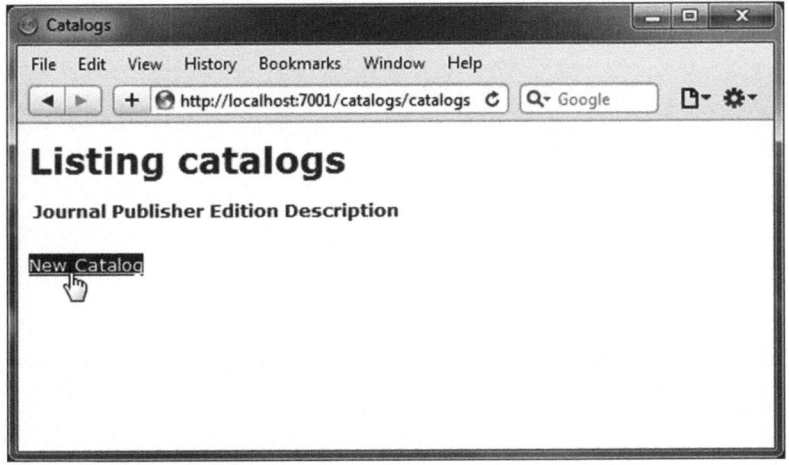

Fig. 11.5 Selecting the New Catalog link

Fig. 11.6   Creating a catalog

Fig. 11.7 Catalog created

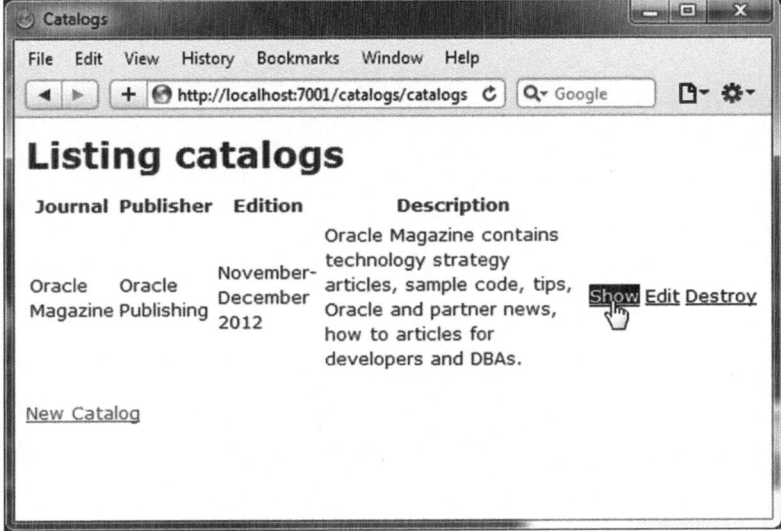

Fig. 11.8 Listing catalogs

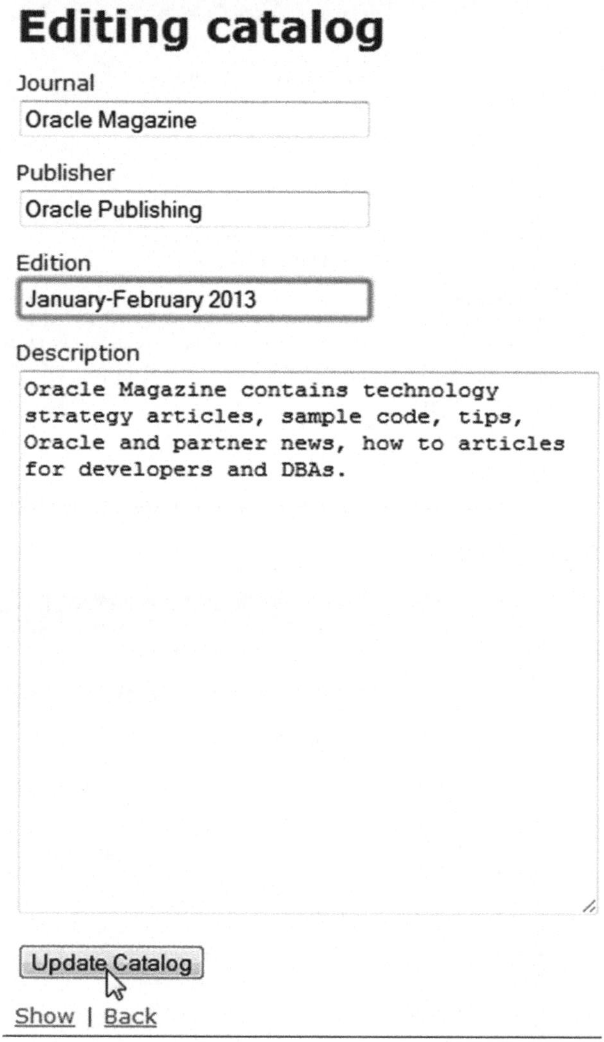

Fig. 11.9 Updating a catalog

Editing catalog

Journal

> Oracle Magazine

Publisher

> Oracle Publishing

Edition

> January-February 2013

Description

> Oracle Magazine contains technology
> strategy articles, sample code, tips,
> Oracle and partner news, how to articles
> for developers and DBAs.

Update Catalog

Show | Back

Chapter 12
Running the Web Application in JBoss™ Application Server 7

In the previous Chap. 11 we deploy and run the JRuby based Web application in Oracle™ WebLogic server. In this chapter we deploy and run the same web application `catalogs.war` in JBoss application server 7, which is the most commonly used open source Java™ EE application server.

12.1   Deploying the Web Application to JBoss AS 7

Start the JBoss AS 7 standalone server. Double click on the `C:\JBossAS7\jboss-as-7.1.1.Final\bin\standalone.bat` file to start the JBoss AS 7 standalone server.

Copy the `catalogs.war` generated with the `warble war` command to the `C:\JBossAS7\jboss-as-7.1.1.Final\standalone\deployments` directory. The directory path to the deployments directory may vary with installation. The `catalogs.war` file gets deployed to the JBoss AS 7 as shown in Fig. 12.1.

12.2   Running the Web Application in JBoss AS 7

Invoke the URL `http://localhost:8080/catalogs/catalogs` in a browser to run the JRuby Rails based web application. The `index.html.erb` gets rendered with a link **New Catalog**. Click on New Catalog to create a new catalog. In the New catalog page an input form is displayed to create a new catalog entry. Add values to catalog entry fields and click on Create Catalog as shown in Fig. 12.2.

A catalog entry gets created as shown in Fig. 12.3. Click on Edit to modify the catalog entry. Click on Back to navigate to the index page.

D. Vohra, *JRuby Rails Web Application Development*, SpringerBriefs in Computer Science,   49
DOI 10.1007/978-3-319-03934-3_12, © The Author(s) 2014

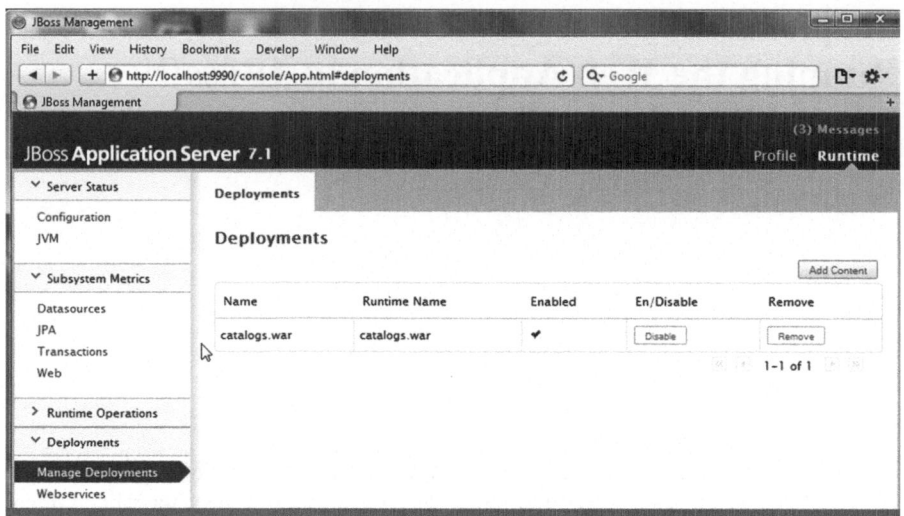

Fig. 12.1 The catalogs.war deployed in JBoss Application Server 7 as shown in the Admin Console

The `deployments` directory is the auto deployments directory for JBoss AS 7. Any WAR file copied to the directory gets installed to JBoss AS 7 when the server is running.

In Chap. 13, we use a JDBC datasource with a JNDI binding instead of a JDBC driver and connection URL in the `database.yml` configuration.

Fig. 12.2 Creating a catalog
in JBoss AS 7

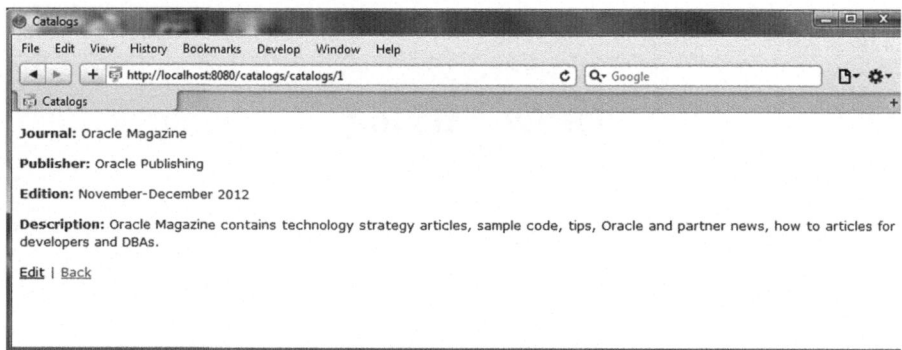

Fig. 12.3 Displaying a catalog in JBoss AS 7

Chapter 13
Using JDBC Data Source with a JNDI

We used connection parameters `driver`, `url`, `username` and `password` in the `database.yml` to configure the production environment database. Alternatively, we may configure the production database as a data source with a JNDI (Java™ Naming and Directory Interface) name in `database.yml`. In this chapter we shall configure a data source in Oracle™ WebLogic Server and use the data source JNDI in the `database.yml` to connect to Oracle™ database.

13.1 Creating a Data Source JNDI in WebLogic Server

In the WebLogic Server select Services|Data sources. Click on New|Generic Data Source to create a new data source as shown in Fig. 13.1.

Specify the **JDBC Data Source Properties**. Specify a data source **Name**, a **JNDI Name (jdbc/OracleDS)** and select **Database Type** as **Oracle**. Click on Next as shown in Fig. 13.2.

Select the default **Database Driver** Oracle's Driver (Thin XA) and click on Next. Select the default **Transaction Options** and click on Next. In Connection Properties specify **Database Name** as **XE**, **Host Name** as **localhost**, **Port** as **1521**, **Database User Name** as **OE** (or a different username) and the **Password**, and click on Next. **Driver Class Name**, **URL**, Database USER Name, and Password get displayed. Click on **Test Configuration** to test the connection. A *Connection test succeeded* message indicates the connection gets established. Click on Next. The AdminServer is listed as the target server. Click on Finish. A data source gets configured as shown in Fig. 13.3.

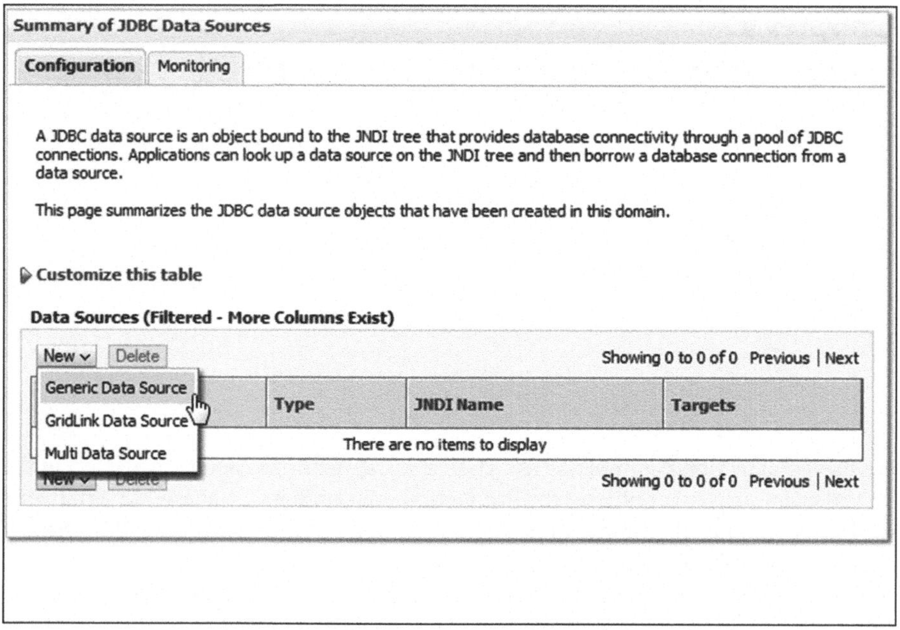

Fig. 13.1 Selecting New > Generic Data Source in WebLogic Server Admin Console

13.2   Configuring the Data Source in Rails Application

To use the data source in the Rails application, configure the production database with the jndi parameter in database.yml.

```
production:
    adapter: jdbc
    jndi: jdbc/OracleDS
```

Repackage the catalogs application with the warble war command. Redeploy the application and run the web application with the same url http://localhost:7001/catalogs/catalogs to display the same index page.

Instead of using a driver, url, username and password parameters we used the jndi parameter to specify a data source JNDI in database.yml. Similarly, a data source JNDI may be configured in JBoss™ AS 7 with MySQL™ database and the JNDI name specified in database.yml.

In Chap. 14 we discuss some of the common issues in developing a JRuby web application and how to fix the issues.

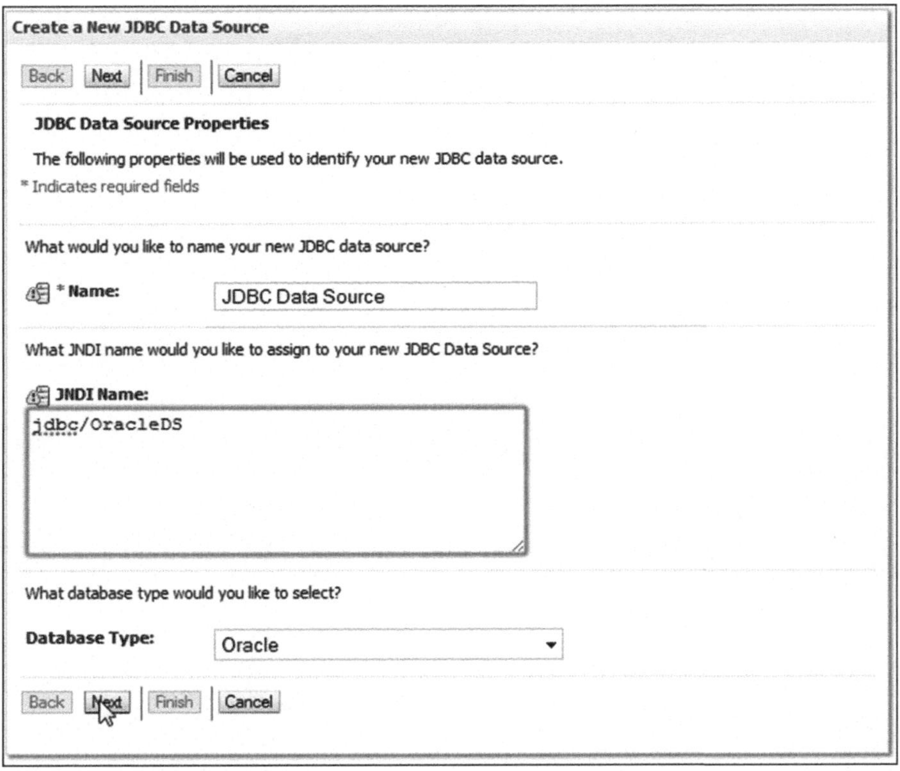

Fig. 13.2 Creating a data source in WebLogic Server

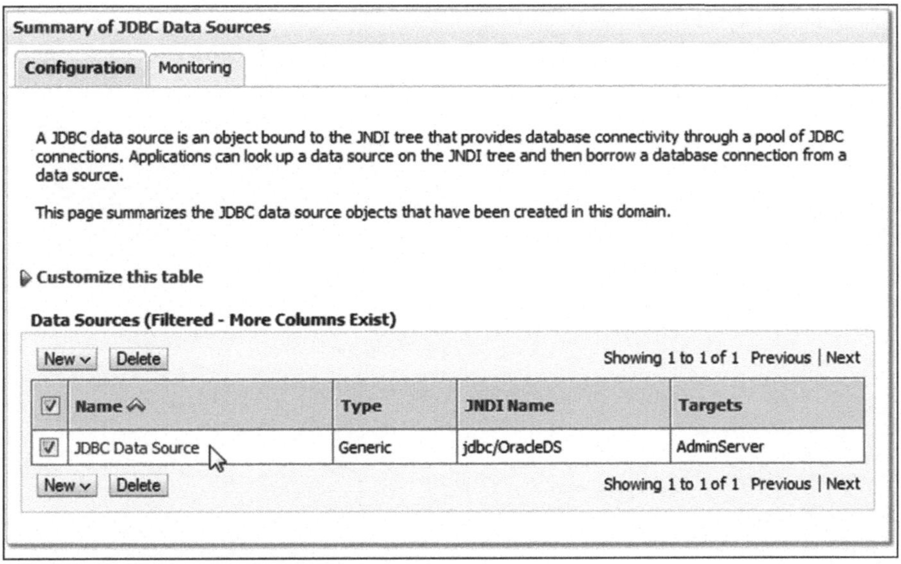

Fig. 13.3 A data source with a JNDI name in WebLogic Server

Chapter 14
Fixing Common Issues in JRuby Web Application Development

In the previous chapters we discussed using JRuby to create a Rails application and deploy the application to Oracle™ WebLogic Server and JBoss™ application server. In this chapter, we will cover the following issues that could occur in developing a JRuby Web application.

- `CLOB` type field
- `jruby.jar` in Classpath
- Adapter not specified
- Driver class and URL not specified
- Driver class not in classpath
- Joda Time version
- Assets precompilation
- Key/Value pairs specified with ':'
- Session store
- Java™ version
- Production database for WebLogic Server
- Development database for rake tasks
- JSON Parameters
- Flash not enabled

14.1 CLOB Type Field

One of the fields (the `description` field) for the `catalogs` table is of type `CLOB`. If Rails 3.2.8 is used instead of Rails 3.1.8 and a new catalog entry created the following error gets generated.

```
NoMethodError in CatalogsController#create
undefined    method    `unserializable_attribute?'    for
#<Catalog:0xc11c0f>
```

D. Vohra, *JRuby Rails Web Application Development*, SpringerBriefs in Computer Science, 57
DOI 10.1007/978-3-319-03934-3_14, © The Author(s) 2014

To fix the error remove Rails 3.2.8 with following commands.

```
gem uninstall rails -v 3.2.8
gem   uninstall   actionmailer   actionpack   activerecord
activesupport activeresource rails -v=3.2.8
```

Download Rails 3.1.8 gem rails-3.1.8.gem from http://rubygems.org/gems/rails/versions/3.1.8. Run the following command from the directory with the rails--3.1.8.gem file.

```
jruby -S gem install rails
```

The issue occurs because the `unserializable_attribute?` is called from the file `activerecord-jdbc-adapter-1.2.2/lib/arjdbc/oracle/adaptor.rb`. `unserializable_attribute?` is defined in `activerecord-3.1.x/lib/active_record/attribute_methods/read.rb`, but not in the 3.2.x version of `read.rb`. The `activerecord-jdbc-adapter` is not updated for Rails 3.2.x.

14.2   jruby.jar in Classpath

In packaging the Rails Application to a Web Application we used warbler to package the Rails application to a WAR file. Warbler includes the `jruby-complete.jar`, which is required for JRuby runtime in the WAR file. If `jruby.jar` is also added in the runtime classpath of WebLogic Server the following error gets generated when the web application is run.

```
file:/C:/jruby-
1.7.0.RC2/lib/jruby.jar!/jruby/jruby.rb:11        warning:
already initialized constant ClassReader
<21-Oct-2012 12:06:55 o'clock PM PDT> <Error> <Servlet-
Context-/catalogs> <BEA-00
0000> <ERROR: application error
org.jruby.rack.RackInitializationException:   uninitial-
ized constant Gem::Config
```

To fix the error remove the `jruby.jar` (C:/jruby-1.7.0/lib/jruby.jar) in the runtime classpath of WebLogic Server. Having jruby runtime JAR in the runtime classpath of the WebLogic server and also as a packaged JAR in the WAR file generates the error. JRuby is getting double-initialized. The JRuby should be assigning the constant `ClassReader` only once.

14.3   Adapter Not Specified

In configuring databases we specified the adapter parameter in database. yml. If the adapter parameter is not specified in database.yml the following error gets generated when a rake command to create or migrate a database is run.

```
rake db:create
rake aborted!
Please install the  adapter: `gem install activerecord-
-adapter` (Exception loading extension `active_record.
connection_adapters.`: java.lang.StringIndexOutOfBo
undsException: String index out of range: 0)
```

To fix the error specify the adapter parameter in the development database in database.yml before running a rake task.

```
development:
  adapter: jdbc
```

The adapter parameter is required to load the activerecord-jdbc- adapter adapter, which is required for ActiveRecord JDBC.

14.4   Driver Class and URL Not Specified

In configuring databases we specified the url and driver parameters in data- base.yml. If the driver and url parameters are not specified the following error gets generated when the rake tasks are run.

```
rake db:create
rake aborted!
jdbc adapter requires driver class and url
```

To fix the error specify the driver and url parameters in the development database in database.yml before running a rake task.

```
driver: oracle.jdbc.OracleDriver
url: jdbc:oracle:thin:@localhost:1521:XE
```

The jdbc adapter requires the driver and url parameters to establish a con- nection with the Oracle™ database.

14.5 Driver Class Not in Classpath

In Chap. 3. we added the `ojdbc6.jar`, which has the driver class for Oracle database, to the `CLASSPATH` environment variable. If `ojdbc6.jar` is not added to the `CLASSPATH` the following error gets generated when rake tasks are run.

```
rake db:migrate
rake aborted!
The driver encountered an unknown error: cannot load
Java class oracle.jdbc.OracLeDriver
```

To fix the error add the `ojdbc6.jar` to the `CLASSPATH` environment variable before running a rake task. The Oracle database JDBC driver class `oracle.jdbc.OracleDriver` is specified in the `driver` parameter value in `database.yml`. When the rake command is run and the driver class is not found the error gets generated; adding the driver JAR to classpath fixes the error.

14.6 Joda Time Version

The Joda Time is required by the JRuby runtime. Joda Time is packaged with the jruby runtime JAR files in the WAR file generated by warbler in packaging the Rails application to a Web application. WebLogic Server includes an old version of Joda Time, which is referenced in the Manifest file of `weblogic.jar`, and thus is higher in the classloader hierarchy than the JAR files packaged in the `catalogs.war` file. When the web application is run on WebLogic Server the Joda Time from the WebLogic Server runtime gets loaded first and generates the following error.

```
ERROR: application error
org.jruby.rack.RackInitializationException: load error:
active_support/core_ext/
time/marshal -- java.lang.NoSuchMethodError: org.joda.
time.DateTime.withYear(I)L
org/joda/time/DateTime;
```

To fix the error add a `weblogic.xml` with `<prefer-web-inf-classes>true</prefer-web-inf-classes>` to the `catalogs.war` as explained in Chap. 11. With the `weblogic.xml` configuration the Joda Time from the jruby runtime packaged in `catalogs.war` gets loaded first. The `withYear` method on `DateTime` was added in a latter version than the Joda Time version in WebLogic Server runtime. The Joda Time version packaged with the `catalogs.war` includes the `withYear` method on `DateTime`. Loading the Joda Time from the WAR file before the Joda Time from the WebLogic Server runtime fixes the error.

14.7   Assets Precompilation

As discussed in Chap. 8 Rails 3.1 uses the Sprockets based "Assets Pipeline" to precompile and merge CSS and JavaScript assets to facilitate running a Rails application. If the assets are not precompiled the following error gets generated.

```
Sprockets::Helpers::RailsHelper::AssetPaths:
:AssetNotPrecompiledError in Catalogs#index
Showing    C:/Oracle/Middleware/user_projects/domains/
base_domain2/servers/AdminServer/tmp/_WL_user/
catalogs/5k0r9w/war/WEB-INF/app/views/layouts/applica-
tion.html.erb where line #5 raised:application.css isn't
precompiled
```

Precompile assets as discussed in Chap. 8 to fix the error. Live compilation, though supported, is not reliable. Precompiling assets ensures that the CSS and JavaScript files are available when the Rails application is run.

14.8   Ruby 1.9.2 Syntax

JRuby 1.7 does not fully support Ruby 1.9.x syntax. Ruby 1.9.2 has introduced a new syntax for hash argument, which may be specified as key: value. The catalogs_controller.rb generates the following error if key/value pairs are specified using ':' instead of '=>'.

```
ERROR: application error
org.jruby.rack.RackInitializationException:  C:/Oracle/
Middleware/user_projects/domains/base_domain/servers/
AdminServer/tmp/_WL_user/catalogs/5k0r9w/war/WEB-INF/
app/controllers/catalogs_controller.rb:9: syntax error,
unexpected ':'format.json { render json: @catalogs }
```

The index.html.erb might generate one of the following error messages.

```
SyntaxError in Catalogs#index
Showing    C:/Oracle/Middleware/user_projects/domains/
base_domain/servers/AdminServer/tmp/_WL_user/
catalogs/5k0r9w/war/WEB-INF/app/views/catalogs/index.
html.erb where line #22 raised:
C:/Oracle/Middleware/user_projects/domains/base_domain/
servers/AdminServer/tmp/_WL_user/catalogs/5k0r9w/war/
WEB-INF/app/views/catalogs/index.html.erb:22:    syntax
error, unexpected ':'
```

```
<td>');@output_buffer.append  =  (  link_to  'Destroy',
catalog, confirm: 'Are you sure?', method: :delete );@
output_buffer.safe_concat('</td>
    ^
```

or

```
undefined local  variable  or  method  `confirm'  for
#<#<Class:0xec1cba>:0x53bc48>
```

Replace ':' with '=>' in key/value pairs in catalogs_controller.rb, index.html.erb. Replace 'confirm' with :confirm in index.html.erb. Making the Ruby scripts syntax as pre Ruby 1.9.2 fixes the error. The undefined local variable or method `confirm' is generated because the reference to confirm is non-specific. Making confirm a symbol with the ':' prefix assigns an internal representation to confirm. Symbols that have been assigned to are treated as variables and un-assigned symbols are method calls.

14.9   Session Store

The session store is used to store flash messages while running and using the Rails application. By default the session store is stored in the WEB-INF/config/initializers/session_store.rb script. The default session store mechanism is cookie store specified with :cookie_store. Cookie store is not the recommended method. If cookie store is used as session store one of the following errors could get generated:

```
ERROR: application error
org.jruby.rack.RackInitializationException:    undefined
local variable or method `key' for main:Object
```

or:

```
<ERROR: application error
org.jruby.rack.RackInitializationException: C:/Oracle/
Middleware/user_projects/domains/base_domain/servers/
AdminServer/tmp/_WL_user/catalogs/5k0r9w/war/WEB-INF/
config/initializers/session_store.rb:3:  syntax   error,
unexpected ':'
Catalogs::Application.config.session_store      :cookie_
store, key: '_catalogs_session'
```

To fix the cookie store errors in session store, comment out the following declaration in config/initializers/session_store.rb.

```
Catalogs::Application.config.session_store      :cookie_
store, key: '_catalogs_session'
```

And, use database as the session store as discussed in enabling Flash. The cookie store syntax errors get removed if cookie store is not used for session store.

14.10   Java Version

If the WebLogic Server domain is created with an older version (1.6.0_29 for example) and the WAR file is created with a latter version (1.7.0_05 for example) the following error gets generated when url `http://localhost:7001/catalogs/catalogs` is invoked.

```
java.lang.UnsupportedClassVersionError: com/sun/management/GarbageCollectionNotificationInfo    :   Unsupported major.minor version 51.0
```

To fix the error use the same version of Java when creating the `catalogs.war` file from the Rails application with the warbler as when creating a WebLogic Server domain. We used Java 1.7.0._05.

A WAR file created with a latter Java version won't run on a WebLogic Server domain created with an earlier Java version. The reverse, WAR file created with an earlier Java version and run on a WebLogic Server domain created with a latter Java version, runs fine.

14.11   Production Database for WebLogic Server

The WebLogic Server requires the production database to be specified in `database.yml` for running a JRuby WAR file. If the production database is not configured in `database.yml` to run the JRuby war file in WebLogic Server the following error gets generated.

```
<ERROR: application error
org.jruby.rack.RackInitializationException:    production
database is not configured
```

To fix the error configure a `production` database in `database.yml` as discussed in Chap. 5. Even if WebLogic Server is started in `development` mode it requires a `production` database for running a Rails application.

14.12   Development Database for Rake Tasks

For running `rake db:` tasks if the `development` database is not configured in `database.yml` the following error gets generated.

```
rake db:migrate
rake aborted!
development database is not configured
```

To fix the error configure a `development` database in `database.yml` as discussed in Chap. 5. For running database migrations and creating a `sessions` table for Flash the `development` database is required.

14.13 JSON Parameters

The `config/initializers/wrap_parameters.rb`, which is used to wrap the JSON parameters hash into a nested hash so that `POST` requests may be sent without a root element, might generate one of the following error messages:

```
<ERROR: application error
org.jruby.rack.RackInitializationException:   C:/Oracle/
Middleware/user_projects/domains/base_domain/servers/
AdminServer/tmp/_WL_user/catalogs/5k0r9w/war/WEB-INF/
config/initializers/  wrap_parameters.rb:  syntax  error,
unexpected ':'
```

or:

```
ERROR: application error
org.jruby.rack.RackInitializationException:  wrong  num-
ber of arguments (0 for 1)
from   C:/Oracle/Middleware/user_projects/domains/base_
d o m a i n / s e r v e r s / A d m i n S e r v e r / t m p / _ W L _ u s e r /
catalogs/5k0r9w/war/WEB-INF/config/initializers/wrap_
parameters.rb
```

As we did not use JSON parameters, comment out the `config/initializers/wrap_parameters.rb` file to fix the error.

14.14 Flash Not Enabled

If the flash is not enabled the following error gets generated.

```
NoMethodError in CatalogsController#update
undefined method `flash' for #<ActionDispatch::Request:0x
144416e>
```

To fix the error enable flash as discussed in Chap. 9. As the flash messages are stored in the session the Rails sessions need to be enabled in the `config/initializers/session_store.rb` file.

In this chapter we discussed some of the common issues that might get generated and how to fix them.

Index